Data

chology.

92-1278
CIP

Maybe
He's Just a
Jerk

It is the policy of William Morrow and Compa
affiliates, recognizing the importance of preser
print the books we publish on acid-free paper,
that end.

Library of Congress Cataloging-in-Publication D

Rosen, Carol
    Maybe he's just a jerk / by Carol Rosen.
        p.   cm.
    ISBN 0-688-11727-9
    1. Love.   2. Mate selection.   3. Men—Ps
4. Interpersonal relations.   I. Title.
HQ801.R69   1992
646.7'7—dc20

Printed in the United States of America

2   3   4   5   6   7   8   9   10

BOOK DESIGN BY JAYE ZIMET

*This book is dedicated to the jerks who
inspired its writing.*

Maybe He's Just a *Jerk*

Maybe He's Just a *Jerk*

.

Carol Rosen

William Morrow and Company, Inc.
New York

It is the policy of William Morrow and Company, Inc., and its imprints and affiliates, recognizing the importance of preserving what has been written, to print the books we publish on acid-free paper, and we exert our best efforts to that end.

Library of Congress Cataloging-in-Publication Data

Rosen, Carol
    Maybe he's just a jerk / by Carol Rosen.
        p.   cm.
    ISBN 0-688-11727-9
    1. Love.   2. Mate selection.   3. Men—Psychology.
    4. Interpersonal relations.   I. Title.
    HQ801.R69   1992
    646.7'7—dc20   92-1278
                                                                    CIP

Printed in the United States of America

        2   3   4   5   6   7   8   9   10

BOOK DESIGN BY JAYE ZIMET

Acknowledgments

I could never have written *Maybe He's Just a Jerk* without the ongoing guidance and support I received from others. From the moment I started promoting the Jerkline and this book, I have received encouragement, and I appreciate all the help people have given me to make this a reality.

I would like to thank those who thought the Jerkline was worth publicizing. In particular, I appreciate the efforts of Mary Beth Beecher, of the *Chicago Heights Star*; Janet Larsen, of the *Joliet Herald*; Molly

•

Acknowledgments

Woulfe, of the Copley News Service; and Eric Fidler, of the Associated Press. I would also like to thank Pat Harper and the editors at *The Southtown Economist*, which was the first newspaper to write a feature about my project, and all of the media personalities who interviewed me and gave me the chance to tell the world about my project.

I am grateful to my family and friends who hung in there and encouraged me through all the difficult times any new author faces, especially my boyfriend, who has endured (and still is enduring) the taunts of his friends who are all asking him, "How many chapters are about *you!*"

I also appreciate the assistance of the National and Illinois Coalition Against Domestic Violence; the Calumet City Public Library; the director of the Battered Women's Shelter, who checked Chapter 8, "The Batterer," to ensure that the information I've provided is correct; and all of the other helping agencies that assisted me in my research for this book.

My literary agent, Meg Ruley, of the Jane Rotrosen Agency, gave me the encouragement I needed to complete the book, and she found a wonderful publisher in William Morrow. My editor, Victoria Klose, has been very supportive to this first author; she has helped me shape and improve the manuscript, so it will be more accessible to women everywhere.

My deepest gratitude goes to the hundreds of

•

Acknowledgments

women who shared their stories with me—those who wrote me or called on the Jerkline. Without them, this book could not have been written. I want them to know their hardships have not been in vain.

Note: All of the names and most of the circumstances of the women in this book have been changed to protect their privacy, and some of the stories are composites.

Contents

Contents

•

Contents

•

Introduction

A Jerk Made Me Do It

I wrote this book because of—what else!—a jerk. While I was with him, he made my life miserable, but for a long time I thought it was my fault. I tried to improve myself by reading the numerous books and magazines that are filled with advice about how to get and keep a man. This is what many women do. We twist ourselves into pretzellike contortions to meet a man's expectations, just to find out after months or years that *he's a jerk and just not worth the effort.*

Introduction

There's nothing wrong with trying to find ways to improve your relationship. But when you're with a jerk—a man who isn't interested in anything but his own needs—it's a waste of time to try.

I'm glad I found out my man was a jerk before I got too involved. But I was still angry about the energy I wasted on a pointless relationship. And as I talked to my friends, I realized I wasn't the only woman who had fallen into this trap. There are a lot of jerks out there, and a lot of women who are furiously trying to please them, even though it's hopeless.

All the books I was reading were devoted to making relationships work. Who reads those books? Women. There were no books that told the truth I had learned—that some men simply aren't worth the effort. So I started a project to get other women talking about their "jerksperiences." I got a post-office box number. Then I called my local newspaper, *The Southtown Economist*. The editors were interested and decided to write a feature story about my project. Before I knew it, the idea caught fire. The Associated Press sent out a news item, and I started getting interviewed by the radio and TV stations in my area. Letters from women across the country flooded into my post-office box.

I could see I was on to something. After three months, I decided to go one step further and start the Jerkline™—a telephone number women could call

•

with their experiences. I was still giving interviews on radio and television stations all over the country, and the calls and letters poured in.

I had hit a nerve. It was very comforting to realize that I definitely was not the only woman who'd had a jerk in her life. I went from having a "cute" idea to having a mission. I wanted to share the stories of the hundreds of women who had contacted me so other women would see that there are jerks out there. I thought if I described some typical jerk behavior, women would recognize it and stop driving themselves crazy trying to please men who could not be pleased. The stories in this book are not by "experts" who tell you their theories. They're by real, live women. We can all learn things from their experiences.

As you read the stories, you may find that you identify strongly with one or more of the women portrayed. If you do, I hope this identification will make you feel less alone and show you that you are not inferior in any way just because you landed a jerk. Almost every woman has had a jerksperience in her life.

I think you'll find a lot of support in this book to help you stop blaming yourself when things go wrong in your relationship. Because *maybe he's just a jerk.*

•

Maybe
He's Just a
Jerk

Chapter One

•

The Relationship from Hell

When Love Becomes a Nightmare

*A*ll our lives we women have been told we're nothing without a man. Not necessarily a great man,
or a kind man, or a loving man—just a man. I have
spoken with hundreds of women who have hung on
to their relationships for dear life. Even when the
guys were Class A jerks, they believed it was better
than being alone. As one woman said, "He may be a
jerk, but he's *my* jerk."

The women who contacted me for this book did all
the usual things women in bad relationships do:

•

- They allowed men to dominate their lives completely, keeping them from developing healthy relationships with family and friends.
- They sacrificed their own needs to meet his. They arranged their lives to make his life easier and more pleasant, repressing their sexual desires to satisfy his.
- They made excuses for terrible behavior, saying, "He didn't really mean it," or, my favorite, "He was under a lot of stress." (Some men have been known to be "under stress" their entire lives!)
- They took all the blame for their bad relationships, saying, "Maybe if I'd been kinder, softer, more understanding, more loving, sexier, prettier . . . ," things would be different.
- They tolerated unbelievable insults to their dignity and self-respect, and kept forgiving their men again and again.

When it came right down to it, however, they had to admit their men were never going to change and would keep on hurting them until the women decided to leave—or were left.

This may sound like a man-bashing book, but it's not. When I was interviewed by television and radio

•

stations about why I started the Jerkline, the male interviewers always tried to find out what my grudge was. I don't have a grudge. In fact, I love men—I'm with a very good one now—but before I found this great guy, I was with a jerk. And my message to women is very simple: You don't have to stay with a jerk. You don't have to tolerate a relationship from hell. Get out, and get on with your life. You'll be happier, and—who knows—once you've left the jerk behind, you might discover there are men out there who don't make your life miserable and destroy your self-esteem. You'll never find Mr. Right if you're stuck with Mr. Wrong.

I'm not saying that your life will be a Cinderella story. Even good relationships have their bad days. That's just the way life is. But life with a jerk is not merely the normal give-and-take that happens in every relationship. It's more bad than good. If the stories I heard are any indication, your life is unhappy most of the time.

How do you know if you're with a jerk? It's not always so easy to tell. Love really *can* be blind. And jerks come in many varieties. Let me give you an idea of the kinds of behavior that might classify a man as a jerk. I've isolated eight types:

•

1. The Critic

This man is never satisfied with anything you do, and he blames you for everything that goes wrong. Maybe he'll say, "So, I'm just a perfectionist," or "What's wrong with having high standards?" But the funny thing is, those "high standards" apply only to you. After all, why should he have to change? He gets much more pleasure out of trying to change you. You could jump through burning hoops with roses in your teeth, and he'd find fault with your form.

A woman with a Critic might drive herself crazy trying to please him. But the terrible truth is, no matter how much you try, he will never be pleased.

Over time, a Critic will beat you down emotionally. Even a woman who has a healthy ego will have trouble maintaining her self-esteem when the person she looks to for approval and love continually finds fault with everything she does. It's inevitable that she'll start doubting herself.

No one, man or woman, is perfect. But for a positive relationship to exist between adults who choose to be with one another, it is necessary for them to accept the fact that adjustments are part and parcel of life. Unfortunately, the Critic believes that change is exactly what is needed to enhance your relationship— as long as *you* are the one doing the changing.

•

2. *The Con Man*

He will come on very strong and sweep you off your feet. Maybe he's the most charming man you've ever met. If you're used to being with men who can't express their feelings, he'll seem like a breath of fresh air. He's not only able to express *his* feelings; he'll express *yours* as well. Suddenly, here's a man who says the things you've always dreamed about hearing—someone who is totally devoted to you.

Once he gets you though, the party's over. He tricks you into loving him, then he begins to take advantage of you. Men like this prey on women who are particularly vulnerable or lonely, and the result is always a nightmare. You lose your money, your home, your security—and, of course, your sanity. These Con Men may not appear on *America's Most Wanted,* but according to the women I interviewed who were conned, there should be a hotline devoted just to them. "Publish his name," one woman urged me. "I don't want the same thing to happen to anyone else."

3. *The Sleazy Lover*

He's God's gift to women—as many women as he can find. He thinks he's Romeo, and every woman is

•

his Juliet. This guy's brain is permanently located in his Fruit of the Looms.

Psychologists would probably say the reason he needs more than one woman is because he's insecure. But it doesn't matter what the reason is for his behavior; it will break your heart. I've never met a woman who wasn't deeply shattered to find the man she loved in the arms of another woman. It's the most intimate form of betrayal.

Once they get caught, Sleazy Lovers are full of excuses and false promises. But there don't seem to be a lot of reformed Sleazy Lovers around. When they make love to a woman, it isn't really love. It's sexual conquest. You're just another notch on their belts.

4. The Charming Scoundrel

This man loves being in love. He's an incredible romantic, until it comes time to make a commitment. Then he'll run as though his pants were on fire. For him, the thrill is in the chase. Once he catches you, he's ready to move on—even if it's right before your wedding day.

The Charming Scoundrel has plenty of reasons for his inability to settle down: He's confused, he's not ready to commit (even if you've been going together

•

for years), he needs to find himself. You try to be understanding and give him time. Whenever you decide enough is enough, he turns on the charm and heats up the romance. The years go by, and he never finds himself or gets more ready to commit. He's a big waste of time.

5. The Married Seducer

He has a line a mile long. He tells you, "You're the only one who makes me happy." Or, "I haven't slept with my wife in years." Or, "I'm married in name only." Or, "In my heart, I'm married to you." Or, the big one, "Be patient. Someday we'll be together." You buy his line, but meanwhile you spend every holiday, every birthday and most nights alone.

He convinces you that his marriage is miserable and only you make him happy. How can you deny him? But the Married Seducer is a great manipulator—and chances are, you're not the first woman he's said these words to. It's a rare married man who leaves his wife and marries his lover. Even if he has a lousy marriage and finally gets a divorce, it's unlikely that he's going to want to settle down right away. What he wants is freedom, and by the time he gets divorced, you don't represent freedom to him anymore.

•

6. The Mama's Boy

When you're with a Mama's Boy, you're always competing, and you'll never win. Remember the song, "I want a girl just like the girl who married dear old Dad?" That's a Mama's Boy. The problem is, that girl does not exist. If you're unlucky enough to be a contender, your life will be an endless series of comparisons, with you the loser.

The Mama's Boy is chronically immature and dependent. If you disappoint him—and, trust me, you will—he'll always return to the safety of his mother. That doesn't necessarily mean he'll go back to her physically; but his heart belongs to her. Their relationship is so tight, there's no room for you.

7. The Batterer

This man is the ultimate controller. If he can't get his way, he uses a fist. He's like the schoolyard bully who wins his arguments by using physical force against smaller kids. With a Batterer, there's no such thing as one slipup. A man who hits you once will hit you again.

The crazy thing about a Batterer is that he'll blame you for his behavior! He'll say, "I couldn't help it.

•

Sometimes you make me so angry." *It's never your fault if a man hits you.*

There are many reasons women stay with men who beat them up. Almost all of the women I talked to told me stories about how loving and sweet their Batterers became after the violence was over. "He was so sorry, I felt terrible for him"—this from a woman who had her shoulder dislocated. Another woman said, "He cried like a baby. I held him for hours. By the time he fell asleep in my arms, I had forgiven him." But the Batterer's tears, like his repentance and promises, are only temporary. Let me state this one more time: *A man who hits you once will hit you again and again and again. . . .*

8. The Addict

This man is in love, but the object of his passion is not you. It's alcohol or drugs. You'll never come first. I was very moved by the story of a woman who gave an ultimatum to her husband: "Choose me or the booze." He shook his head sadly, and said, "I'm sorry. . . ." She left him the next day.

Drug or alcohol addiction is a disease, and we can feel compassion for those who have the sickness. But the point is, no woman has to stick around to play

•

nurse and keeper to a drunk or a drug addict. The addiction dominates a relationship and will soon destroy not only your partner's life, but your own.

Why do women stay with jerks? It's very hard for an outsider to understand. There were times during my research when even though I was a veteran of a bad relationship, I wanted to say, "Wake up and smell the coffee! Dump the bum." However, I realized that it's easy for people outside a relationship to see the truth, but it's different from the inside. The women you will meet in this book are not unusually foolish or dense. They're just like you and me. Many of them are highly educated and self-assured—the last people you'd ever expect to find in abusive relationships. Every single one of them deserves better than she got, but sometimes it takes a long time to figure that out.

This book is a wake-up call for all the women who have loved and been hurt. It's also a warning to jerks: We know who you are and we aren't going to take it anymore!

•

Chapter Two

·

The Critic

He Blames You
for Everything

"*E*veryone can do everything better than me,"
Joanna said when she called the Jerkline.
"That's what it's like being married to Kyle. It never
stops. When I cook, he says that So-and-so is a better
cook. When I sew, So-and-so is a fabulous seamstress.
If he can't perform in bed, it's because I'm a lousy
lover—unlike So-and-so.

"So-and-so can be anyone—his mother, his ex-
girlfriend, a co-worker. It doesn't matter. The point

·

is, I can't measure up. He makes me feel like a loser every single day."

Joanna is married to a Critic. She could be perfect, and it still wouldn't matter. With a Critic, you can never do anything right.

I understood what Joanna was going through. I had been in a relationship with a Critic, and it took me a long time to realize that I was a victim of psychological abuse. I thought I was the "bad person" in the relationship. He had me so convinced everything was my fault that for a long time I didn't even confide in my closest friends.

Finally, I broke down. After one particularly nasty verbal tirade, when he called me every name in the book and attacked every aspect of my character, I called my friend Karla, crying. When I told her what happened, she said, "That's mental cruelty!"

"Huh?" I was so convinced I was doing something wrong that it had never occurred to me it might be him. Karla and I talked for a while, and I began to see that it was abuse. It had been going on for more than a year, and it was getting worse all the time.

After my heart-to-heart discussion with Karla, I began to take a long, hard look at my relationship with this man. I noticed that he was always bad-mouthing people, especially my friends. I discovered he had been bullying people since he was a little boy. Knowing these things about him allowed me to be

•

more objective about his behavior. It got to the point that when he began one of his now-familiar tirades, I could just sit back and think, This guy really can't control himself. He's the one with the problem, not me.

That was the beginning of my healing, but it took time. At first I thought if I confronted him with his negative behavior and tried really hard, the relationship could be saved, because there were positive things, too. But I finally admitted that it didn't matter how hard I tried; the good spells were becoming shorter and shorter. No matter what I said, his opinion remained the same. He didn't think he was being abusive. He felt his actions, attitudes and behaviors were completely on target. I realized he wasn't going to change. If I stayed, I could expect the same and maybe worse. I chose to keep my sanity, dignity and self-respect intact. He couldn't understand when I told him the relationship was over. It was hard at first, but after a few weeks, I realized I had done the right thing.

You may be in a similar situation—feeling put down and upset all the time but not understanding why. That's one of the major reasons I felt compelled to write this book. My own experience and the stories of women who wrote to me and called the Jerkline have helped me understand the typical patterns of the Critic. See if you can relate to any of these:

•

Carol Rosen

He Controls Your Life

Controlling behavior takes many forms. Some of them seem innocent, and even loving. He might say, "Honey, why don't you quit your job? You deserve a break, and you have me to take care of you." When a controlling man says this, it isn't because of love or concern for your welfare. He's looking for power. Women have told me about quitting their jobs, only to find themselves put on measly weekly allowances, or having their husbands say, "The one who brings home the bacon makes the rules."

Financial control is one of the main ways that some men keep women under their thumbs. If you're married to a man who makes you beg for every penny and uses money to hold you in line, I strongly urge you to try to get some financial independence—even if it means taking a job for a few hours every week. If you have small children, you can begin to upgrade your skills while they're still at home by taking a class or two so that you'll be ready to get a job when they start school. I've heard from women who have formed baby-sitting cooperatives to help each other pursue their interests. This is important if you're with a controlling jerk. A normal, loving man will mean well when he offers to support and take care of you. But a jerk's motives aren't loving. He wants to make sure you stay dependent upon him.

•

Another way some men control women is by trying to limit their access to family and friends. This also seems quite innocent in the beginning. You might tell him you've planned to have dinner with a girl-friend you haven't seen for a while, and he'll pout and say, "Oh, honey, I thought we'd just relax and watch videos tonight. It's so great when we're together— wouldn't you rather stay with me?" You feel guilty and also a little flattered. He loves you so much he can't stand to be without you. But his desire to have you with him isn't about love; it's about control.

He might also begin to criticize your family and friends: "It wasn't very nice of Rhonda to snap at you that way." Or, "Boy, your dad sure is set in his ways, isn't he?" If you're really insecure, he'll soon have you questioning all of your relationships—except the one with him. He'll convince you that he's the only one you can trust; he's your best friend. "Don't worry, honey," he'll assure you. "They may not treat you right, but I'll always be here for you."

If his ploy works, you'll soon find that you are becoming isolated and estranged from everybody you care about. He wants you to think your world revolves around him. And eventually it becomes true. Your life is centered on him. That's what happened to one woman who wrote:

•

Terri's Isolation

From the first week I knew him, John began to alienate me from my family and friends— and even from my own children. I was too blind to see what was happening. I allowed him to complain about everyone to the point that I just stopped seeing them. I figured if I stayed away from them, he wouldn't have any reason to complain.

My teenage children lived with my ex-husband across town, and when they came to see me, John nagged them constantly about the food they ate, their choice of music, their supposed lack of appreciation for all the things he said he'd done for them and anything else he could think of. He resented my spending time with them or trying to make their visits more enjoyable and always found ways to put me down in front of them. They finally found excuses to stay away. I didn't blame them, but it broke my heart.

But even keeping you to himself isn't enough for the controlling Critic. He'll have you jumping all the time. You try to please him, but it's never enough. This letter is from a woman who left her controlling

•

man five years ago, but she's still mad when she remembers what he did to her:

Donna and the Control Freak

Talk about jerks! About five years ago, I was
with a guy who was emotionally abusive.
Everything started out nice and sweet, and he
behaved like he really cared about me. Then
one day, out of the blue, he accused me of
going out with my friends only so I could find
other men. What I was supposed to do with
all these other men I have no idea. Then I
went to a concert with a girlfriend, and when
she dropped me off, there he was, skulking
around outside my house, accusing me of
lying to him. He was positive I had actually
been out with another man! He said my friend
was just a coverup for my sluttish activities.

I should have seen what he was doing, but
instead I felt sorry for him. I thought he was
just insecure, and I figured I could show him
by my love that he had nothing to worry
about. I let him move in with me, but things
got worse. He constantly criticized and
whined about everything until I couldn't stand
it anymore. Like my bathroom habits. He'd

•

go, "God, why do you have to leave your maxi-pads in the trash? Why don't you take them outside or something? Gross!" I finally made him move out. Then came the final blow. I received a phone call from him at five A.M. on a Sunday morning asking where the hell I'd been all night. It turns out he'd slept in his car outside of my home. Just because I didn't notice he was parked there and come to the door, he assumed I had been with another man. Give me a break!

He Demands Perfection

With the perfectionist, you may look like Raquel Welch, cook like Julia Child, and perform in bed like the Happy Hooker, but he'll still find something to criticize.

This is a game in which, no matter what you do, you won't make the right choice. As that wonderful Gilda Radner character Rosanne Rosanna-Dana used to say on *Saturday Night Live,* "It's always something."

The perfectionist will nag you to death. It's like the ocean battering a rock. Ultimately, the ocean will erode the rock. A nagger will find a fault and pick at it endlessly: "You were really loud at the party last

•

night." "You're wearing too much makeup." "That dress makes you look fat."

Eventually, you'll be afraid to breathe the wrong way, because he might bitch about it. That's the way Mary felt:

Mary and the Chauvinist

The term "jerk" is an understatement when it comes to my husband. He is sometimes the sweetest man alive, but you would have to experience everyday life with him to believe it. He will sit on his skinny little butt and complain about our messy house, while his contribution consists only of sarcastic comments about how I could keep it cleaner. He says I just don't care enough about our home. This is the same man who will call the dog over, put his dinner plate on the floor, and let the mutt devour what is left of his food. Then he'll get up and walk away, leaving his plate on the floor. We own our own business and work side by side every day, so I get no relief from his primitive, male-chauvinist attitudes. He makes his motto clear: "No dick, no brains; no exceptions."

At times I would like to permanently shut him up. He will stand behind me when I cook

•

and instruct me on how he thinks it should be done. This is very brave when you consider that I often have a sharp knife in my hand. Maybe someday I'll turn around real fast and give him a little carving lesson. That would shut him up!

He Neglects You

As bad as direct abuse is, neglect can be just as harmful. Sometimes a Critic controls you by treating you like a piece of furniture. This letter brought tears to my eyes:

The Indifferent Husband

I am a retired college professor who has been putting up with neglect for years. My husband has never given me a birthday card or a Christmas gift in all the years we've been married. He's from Latin America, and he always says, "We don't do that in my country." I have overlooked this, although it was very difficult at first. Until last year, I always got him cards on important days, and usually gifts as well.

Recently, on my sixty-sixth birthday, we attended the wedding of friends, and Robert's

•

behavior was typical. At the reception, after we'd been seated for a while, I asked Robert to get me a glass of punch. All of the other men at our table were bringing punch to their wives. Robert didn't even dignify my request with a reply, much less do it. After an embarrassing wait of ten minutes or so, I got up to get the punch myself. When the photographer came around to take pictures of the guests at our table, we all stood at her request—except Robert. He refused to get up and have his picture taken with the group and made it plain he thought the whole thing was stupid. By the way, although it was my birthday, he never mentioned it. He didn't even wish me a happy birthday.

I was infuriated and embarrassed by his behavior. It was the last straw. When we got home, I demanded that he go with me to a marriage counselor. At first he refused, but later he consented to go. We went only twice, and it was a disaster. He was not cooperative, and he got up and walked out when the counselor suggested ways to make our marriage stronger.

I am about to call it quits. I am not a nagging wife, and I give him no reason to behave this way. All I want is a peaceful, happy life.

•

I've usually overlooked Robert's abusive behavior, but it's getting harder. I do know one thing: I will never spend another birthday with him. This year I'm leaving for England the day before my birthday, and I'm going alone.

Being a martyr is another way the jerk neglects you. It doesn't matter what you're going through, it's nothing compared to his problems. Everything is always about him.

Here's a typical martyr scenario: You have just had a tough day at the office, or the kids have been driving you crazy. Wearily, you throw some hamburgers on the stove. Your husband walks in, lets out a deep sigh, and says, "Is it too much to expect a decent dinner waiting for me after I've worked all day? Is it so hard for you to keep the kids under control so I can have a little peace and quiet?" You might tell him that your day was no picnic either, but he'll always have a list of reasons why his day was worse. Then he'll sulk for the rest of the evening, week, month and, indeed, for the rest of your life.

He Belittles You

A writer friend had just published her first short story. As we celebrated with a bottle of wine, she said,

•

"Carol, I'm glad I can at least celebrate my accomplishment with you. Hal [her boyfriend and an aspiring author] has been vicious ever since I got published. I think he's angry with me because somebody likes my writing. He actually said the magazine that accepted my story was known for its poor editorial standards, which I thought was a pretty crummy thing to say."

One woman told me that her husband used to say, "Paula, you don't have a chest, and you're so skinny the only thing you can do to please me is to use your mouth." He told her he only married her because there were no prettier girls around. He humiliated her and went so far as to yell at her from the bedroom while she was watching TV with the kids, "Paula, are you going to come up here and take care of me or what?" Paula finally left him, but she still has nightmares about him, and she doesn't date because she's afraid of being dominated again.

A favorite way men belittle women is to compare them to others. No matter what you do, his mother/sister/ex-girlfriend did it better. One Jerkline caller told me she got so fed up with being compared to her boyfriend's ex that she finally screamed at him, "If she's so great, go back to her!" Then she walked out.

•

Carol Rosen

He Bullies You

My Critic boyfriend liked to accuse me of making him screw up. Nothing was his fault. It was always me. For example, he hated my cigarette smoking. One day I was smoking in the living room of my home, and he came barreling into the room, screaming that I was choking him to death, and he couldn't breathe. As he pulled up the window, he knocked a plant onto the floor. It was a real mess. He got furious at me: "If you hadn't been smoking, I wouldn't have done that."

This happened all the time. He manipulated me into thinking it was my behavior that made him angry or caused him to screw up. Many women wrote or called to tell me about men who bullied them in this way. Here's Tanya's story:

Tanya's Intimidation

Ted had been at it ever since he was a young boy in Scotland, where he was the neighborhood bully. His girlfriend back home, who had been with him for eight years, almost left her family and church for him. But he called off the wedding shortly before the date and left the country.

When I met him, he was working as an

•

engineer at a nuclear-power plant. I was immediately attracted to him. He was handsome, athletic, smart and filled with self-confidence. He was so charming and so manipulative he could convince you black was white. I gave up everything for him, which is what he demanded, since he was an incredible chauvinist. He believed that women are only good for cooking, cleaning, child raising and screwing, and that they're all money-grubbing parasites. He never baby-sat the children or paid any attention to them, except when it suited his interest. He often said that homemakers, such as myself, were worthless.

We were married for twelve years, after living together for six. I excused his bullying behavior countless times. His mode of operation was intimidation and confrontation. In fact, it was a confrontation with his boss that caused him to lose his job. Being out of work made him more of a bully than ever. I finally told him I wanted a divorce, and he threatened to cut me off financially—of course, all our assets were in his name.

This began a divorce war with no holds barred on his part. He found a way to tie up our funds, so the children and I had nothing. He managed to tie up the title to our house

•

and told me I'd never get it as part of the settlement. With the help of my parents, we finally moved into an apartment. After the divorce, he sealed up the house and moved to another state, so getting the monthly child-support check was nearly impossible.

The final blow came when I discovered he'd had a mistress for four years. He'd promised her a house and had bought her things with our money.

It was a nightmare. Now I'm trying to put my life back together. I'm going back to school and working part time. But I have no interest in socializing or meeting another man.

Another woman wrote of her husband's set of one-sided rules:

Kip's Rules

Kip was very proficient at mental and verbal abuse. If he'd been able to have his way, he'd have had me believing I was responsible for all the world's woes.

Kip's rules were simple: Nothing was ever his fault, he was Number One and he was never wrong.

•

I had to put up with this even after we got divorced. He was irresponsible but never took the blame. It wasn't his fault that he didn't pay the kids' school tuition. It wasn't his fault when they were having trouble with their grades. He was a typical "Disneyland dad," who was around for fun but never helped with the serious stuff. It would never occur to him to check their homework or to help them. He does his time with them like it was a prison sentence, and then he blames me and them when things go wrong.

The first step in handling a Critic is to build your self-esteem, so that you will learn to love and respect yourself again. You may have lost track of what is real and what isn't—especially if you've totally bought his line. You have to realize that often the Critic's statements are ridiculous, and you are a worthwhile person who deserves to be treated with respect. Only when you believe this can you stand up to the Critic and say, "I will no longer allow you to treat me so poorly." If there is a real problem to discuss (as opposed to one that he has manufactured), you can then say, "When you're ready to have a rational discussion, let me know."

I'm warning you, he isn't going to like it. If he's like my boyfriend, he may have the verbal equivalent

•

of an epileptic seizure. Or he may resort to bullying you. Men like this play on your paranoia. He may imply that mutual friends or family members have confided in him that they don't trust your judgment or are worried about your emotional state. One woman who called the Jerkline in tears said that when she stood up to her husband, he threatened to have her declared mentally unfit and unable to take care of their children. Another said her husband threatened to throw her and the kids out of the house without a penny.

One woman's story was particularly horrifying. She had lost a breast to cancer, and her husband used that to keep her in control. If she stood up to him, he reminded her, "You're only half a woman now. No other man will want you, so you'd better be glad you have me."

If it's still early in the relationship, you can nip the behavior in the bud by immediately saying, "I won't tolerate this" when he starts to criticize you unreasonably. Then one of two things will happen. If your Critic is not a "hard-core" emotional abuser, he may cease and desist and act like a decent human being. Or he'll end the relationship. Either of these alternatives is preferable to spending months, years or a lifetime with someone who will tear you apart and destroy your ego.

You may not be lucky enough to be in the early

•

stages of an emotionally abusive relationship. You may have been dating or married to your Critic for years and even have children with him. In that case, there are no instant fixes. You can't always just walk away. You may be financially dependent or very attached to your partner and still believe that one day he'll realize how cruel he's been to you and apologize. In fact, if you have been in a long relationship with a Critic, you can probably remember many instances when he showed remorse. It might even have been quite romantic—with him begging you for forgiveness and telling you he couldn't live without you. For all his apologies and pledges of undying love, however, you've found that nothing has changed for long.

When you finally decide you've had enough and stand up to him, it can be a very satisfying experience. I laughed and applauded when Suzanne called the Jerkline to tell me how she had given her Critic a taste of his own medicine:

Suzanne's Comeback

I was going with a man who just couldn't get off the subject of my bottom teeth. He was such a perfectionist! My teeth are slightly crooked, but it's no big deal, and no one else has ever mentioned them before. But he'd say, "You're beautiful and sensuous—except for

•

your bottom teeth." I swear, he'd bring it up weekly, daily, three times a day, until it drove me crazy. Finally, I'd had it, and I screamed, *"I will fix my teeth when you get a larger penis!"*

I haven't heard from him since.

•

Chapter Three

•

The Con Man

He Tricks You into
Loving Him

When Serina met Harry she was very well off, earning six figures a year as a successful stock-broker. When she called the Jerkline, she described herself as a smart woman who knew what she wanted. "He seemed like a perfectly acceptable partner for a modern woman like me. He looked like he'd just stepped out of a tennis ad. He was charming, absolutely gorgeous, and he treated me like a princess. Nothing was too much. On only our second date, he

•

handed me a box which contained a diamond and sapphire ring with a matching necklace."

Their courtship was fast and incredibly romantic. They spent many evenings at Harry's downtown penthouse, sipping champagne and discussing their future. After six weeks, Harry proposed, and Serina said yes.

"I knew it was fast," she told me, "but it seemed so right, and I didn't want to risk letting this perfect man get away. I'd already been through a divorce, and I never thought I'd have a second chance. Harry was my second chance, and I was determined to have him."

The wedding was a lavish black-tie affair, with the guests transported to the reception by horse-drawn carriages. The blissful couple spent their honeymoon on a Princess cruise. Serina told me, "It was a beautiful time—sunlit days and starlit nights."

At first the marriage was all Serina had dreamed it would be. But before long, Harry started showing small signs of control. He pressured her to sell her antique furniture because he hated antiques. He made her sell her BMW, saying, "It's expensive to maintain and I'll take you anywhere you want to go." He became very jealous every time she had lunch with another man—even though such lunches were a part of her business as a stockbroker.

Next he convinced her to combine their checking

•

accounts. Although he had some money of his own, most of the money in the account was Serina's. Soon his daughter's college tuition and his ex-wife's alimony payments were coming out of Serina's money. He also persuaded Serina to sell her city apartment and country house in order to buy a lavish mansion for them to live in. The mansion was purchased in both their names, although Serina put up the money.

Once Harry had achieved his objectives, his behavior toward Serina began to change. He became moody and critical, and soon they were fighting constantly. Finally, Harry asked for a divorce.

Serina was at her wit's end. "Fine," she screamed at him, "but what am I supposed to do with this goddamn mausoleum?"

"Sell it," Harry answered.

The divorce was a bitter one, with Harry fighting Serina every step of the way over property and assets. It didn't matter that she had footed the bill for everything. Now he had a right to half, and maybe more.

"I got conned," Serina admitted, with a pained sigh. "I thought I was smarter than that, but as they say, love is blind. I just didn't see it. Harry was such a charmer, such a lovely man. It never occurred to me that he could be deceiving me."

"Scam artists," "swindlers" and "flimflam men" are common terms used for the same seedy animal—the

•

53

Con Man. Con Men are experts at ripping women off. They target women who are lonely or vulnerable. They attend singles events, self-help groups or AA programs, and sometimes even scan the obituaries looking for recent widows.

They will use the promise of love to bilk you out of your house, your money and, finally, your sanity. Kim, a woman who called the Jerkline, got wise to her Con Man before he did any damage—although her experience is rare.

"Jared was from another country, and when I realized he just wanted to get married so he could get a green card, I threw the engagement ring back in his face," Kim said. "I didn't hear from him for seven weeks. Then he called and said, 'I'll tell you where I've been. I paid a girl to marry me.' "

Kim began to laugh as she told the story. "I thought it was so funny—and part of it was relief that I hadn't been the one to get suckered. Then he had the nerve to say to me, 'This is just business. I still love you.' Needless to say, I never spoke to him again."

Unfortunately, the way the letters and calls to the Jerkline tell the tale, most women who get involved with Con Men aren't so lucky. The following stories show how men tricked women into loving and caring for them, then took them for all they could get. As you'll see, Con Men don't just go after rich women. Most of the women in these stories were ordinary,

•

hardworking people who were duped out of what little they had.

A Coast-to-Coast Scam

When I met Stan, I was working and he was still in school. He was a very bright man, and I could tell he had a great future ahead of him. He was very sweet and loving. Unlike most men I'd known, Stan didn't mind spending hours being romantic and talking about the future. One thing led to another, and soon I was helping him out financially. I paid our rent, kept the refrigerator stocked and even bought his underwear for him. I didn't mind because I knew everything would even out once he graduated and got work.

Then I got a great job offer in California, and Stan and I decided it would be good for both of us if I accepted it. He would stay in Massachusetts and finish school, then join me there. We parted tearfully, with Stan professing his undying love for me.

While I was in California, I continued to send Stan money. He called me every day—collect, of course—and we had long, love-filled conversations. Everything seemed wonderful until my world was shattered by a

•

phone call from Stan's mother. She said, "Marge, I can't take this anymore. I have to tell you that my son is lying to you. He's not going to school, and he's living with another woman."

I was heartbroken, especially when I discovered that Stan and the woman were planning to get married. I tried to go on with my life. All in all, I figured Stan had conned me out of ten thousand dollars. But worse than that, he'd made it almost impossible for me to ever trust another man. It was a long time before I dated, and even then I was very careful. Now I'm going out with a decent man, and I'm beginning to heal. For a long time, I wanted to hurt Stan, to make him pay for what he did to me. Now I just want to forget him and get on with my life.

The following story is a classic example of a man who was in it for the money. He had no qualms about dumping one woman for another if it meant improving his financial status:

The Cake Caper

Anne met Joe when both of them were on vacation. He was overweight but nice, and they had a good

•

time. When they returned home, they stayed friends, platonically, for a long time before things got serious. Anne was finally ready to admit she was in love. But right before the wedding, Joe broke things off. He admitted he'd been seeing another woman whose father owned a prosperous cake company. Anne told me tearfully when she called the Jerkline, "He said, 'Anne, I love you, but I just have to go with the woman who has the most money.'

"Carol," Ann said, "I was just brokenhearted. I almost had a nervous breakdown over this. To make matters worse, he kept calling me for about a year, telling me I was the one he loved, but he had to go for the money. I'm still wondering if he ate up all the profits."

Con Men have no scruples. If they get caught, they show no remorse. It's amazing how the sweetest guy in the world can become, overnight, the worst creep imaginable. Listen to this story:

Martha and the Corrupt Cop

I started dating Jerry when I was working part time as a security guard. He was a cop, and we hit it off right away. We started dating, and he immediately got involved in my family life. I thought it was sweet how interested he

•

was in everything about us. Now I see he was just casing things.

I lived with my parents, who are elderly. Sometimes Jerry would visit. I kicked him out the day I caught him going through Mom's jewelry, but it was too late. My mom's wedding ring and a few other pieces were missing. So were my dad's credit cards and some cash. My dad put a stop on the credit cards, and I called Jerry at work. When I threatened to press charges, he laughed and said, "Go ahead and call the cops. Who's going to believe you? I am a *cop*." Carol, I was so frustrated I could have screamed. So much for law and order.

Many of the letters and calls I received about Con Men were from older women. Older women are easy targets. They may be lonely or very trusting. I felt outraged when I read Janet's story:

The Condo Cheat

I am a widow with a twenty-year-old daughter. Tom was a widower, and we were in love. There were no fireworks, but we were comfortable together. He moved in with me and my daughter, and we lived happily together for two years.

•

Maybe He's Just a Jerk

After Tom retired, I put my house in New York up for sale, and we decided we would buy a condo together in Maryland. I sold my house and quit my job and put the money down on the condo. Although I arranged for the mortgage, I put Tom's name on the deed. I loved and trusted him, and I never realized I would live to regret it.

Tom knew that my daughter would continue to live with us for a while—she was only eighteen at the time. There had never been any question about it—until we were living in the condo. Then he decided he didn't want my daughter around anymore. When I refused to ask her to move out, he went to a lawyer and tried to have her vacated from the premises. I didn't know anything about it until my daughter and I received a letter from his lawyer in the mail. This may sound crazy, but I swear it happened.

Things got so ugly that I ordered him to leave, but there was one catch: I had put his name on the deed. It's been eight months, and he won't budge, and now my only recourse is to take him to court. I know I'll end up losing the condo, and all that I've worked so hard for.

I'm living in hell. I sleep on the couch be-

•

cause I won't share a bed with him, and the tension is ridiculous. I have no idea why he is doing this and why he won't leave. He has totally cured me of my fear of being alone. I'll never trust a man again. Never.

One brand of Con Man is the user. This man doesn't rip you off in any specific way. He just takes and takes and never gives anything back. Women in these relationships become like slaves carrying all the burdens. Why do they do it? Love, of course—and need. One woman who called the Jerkline admitted she let a man use her because "I was so lonely when I met him. He was loving and affectionate, and I desperately needed to be close to someone. So I let him do it."

Most of the women in the following stories wised up eventually, but not before a lot of damage had been done.

The Dreamer

Boy, do I have a jerk for you! His name is Tony, and we lived together for three years. During that time, he changed jobs at least twice a year and was out of work at least three months out of twelve. During his periods of

•

unemployment, I would work two or three jobs to pay the bills. Even when he did work, he didn't contribute much because he said he had so many personal debts.

Tony was a dreamer—one of those guys who goes for the get-rich-quick schemes. During our relationship, he talked me into fronting him several thousand dollars for various "business" deals that never panned out.

He used me until greener pastures came along. Now he's with someone else who has more money to finance his schemes than I did. It's been a very expensive lesson for me to learn.

The Freeloader

We were scheduled to go out on a date Friday, but he called me at work and said he was really tired, so would I mind if he came to my place, ordered a pizza, and watched videos. I said sure, and we had a nice evening. He even paid for the pizza, so I can't totally complain about that night.

But from that point on, our "dates" were always at my house, with me cooking dinner. "I haven't had a home-cooked meal in ages"

•

was his plaintive cry. After about a month of home-cooked meals, I asked him if we could go out to dinner for a change. He said he thought things were fine just the way they were. When he called to confirm our next date, I told him I was going out to dinner without him—for the rest of my life!

Mr. Cheapskate

I was engaged to a man who was well off financially, but you'd never know it by the way he lived. Although he owned two farms and a lucrative business, he lived in a shabby apartment—and then moved in with me as soon as he could. While he was living with me, he never offered to help with the bills or any of the finances, except to take me out to dinner once in a while.

After he'd lived with me for two months, I asked him to start contributing his share toward the bills. He haggled about it and put me on the defensive. I kicked him out when he had not given me a dime after three months. What a cheapskate!

•

The "Brilliant" Artist

A caller to the Jerkline said:

I just have to tell you about my sister's husband. I can't stand him. She's been supporting
him for twenty-eight years. He's supposedly a
"genius," but I think his art is pathetic. When
he first moved in with my sister, he quit his
job and allowed her to support him while he
puttered around in his studio. She works full
time but still has to cook dinner for him when
she gets home. He's forty-six years old, and
has never sold any of his art or earned a penny
to contribute to their household. He's a bum,
but my sister is his slave.

Bart's Bogus Disability

My husband, Bart, had one main goal in life:
to be on permanent disability while I worked
to support him in high fashion. He even told
me once that he wanted to be temporarily
comatose so I'd have to wipe his butt for him!

Bart had eighteen jobs in twenty-six years.
He found so many ways to be fired and obtain
unemployment or disability that he could
write a how-to book.

•

He controlled me completely and told other people I was stupid or worthless. He'd say, "Someday I'm going to find a rich bitch to support me."

I couldn't leave him because I'm a devout Catholic, but he finally left me after the children were grown. I guess he's found that rich woman. Meanwhile, I should feel lucky to be rid of him, but he's ruined my life, and I'm not sure I'll ever recover.

If you're really unlucky, your Con Man is a bona fide criminal. The clues are there, if you're paying attention. Unfortunately, Rita, a woman who told her story on the Jerkline, missed the obvious clues about her boyfriend, Ed:

The Delinquents

Rita had been going out with Ed for six months when disaster struck. She told me on the Jerkline, "Carol, I knew his friends were delinquents, but he didn't seem at all like them. Ed was different."

Or so she thought:

One day Ed asked me to come over and pick him up at his house; his car was in the shop. He asked, "Is it okay if I bring a friend with

•

me?" I agreed, although I didn't care for his friends.

When we got to my house, Ed took me into the bedroom so we could "talk," leaving his friend in my living room. I wasn't even suspicious, which shows how dumb I was. I should have guessed that something was up.

After our visit, I drove them back to Ed's house. I noticed that Ed's friend sat with his coat draped over his lap, but, again, I didn't think anything of it.

The next morning I went to turn on my VCR to record a program. There was only one problem: The VCR was missing! I knew immediately what had happened. While Ed and I were in the bedroom, his friend unplugged the VCR and put it outside the window. When we left the apartment, he wrapped it in his coat while my back was turned. But that isn't even the worst of it. I found one of my kitchen knives under my couch, and I wondered if Ed's friend was planning to use it if I caught him.

I called Ed, and of course he denied everything. I told him I never wanted to see him again. About a year later, I learned that Ed was in jail for grand larceny. I am so lucky I got out of that relationship!

•

Carol Rosen

A person doesn't have to be a crook to classify as a Con Man. He might just be a man who chronically deceives you about everything and turns out not to be who he says he is. That's what happened to the women in the following stories:

Liar, Liar

Michael was my lawyer about four years ago in a child-support case. We got along great; he had a wonderful sense of humor, was kind, considerate and extremely good-looking. We lost touch after the case, and I was disappointed about that. Then last year, I ran into Michael when he was jogging a few blocks from my house. We started dating, which made me very happy. Within only a few weeks, he was talking about marriage. Even my children loved him.

Then I started noticing some discrepancies. Michael had told me that in addition to practicing law, he taught night classes at the local college. That was his excuse for being gone during the evenings. But once when I tried to reach him at school, I was told there was no record of his working there. I also thought it was strange that after a few months I had not met any of his family or friends.

•

66

Michael started disappearing for long periods of time, and he always had an elaborate excuse. Once when he stood me up for a date, he claimed to have been beaten and robbed. He even went so far as to wear an eye-patch because he said he got glass in his eye when the mugger broke his car window. Oddly, the eye injury cleared up in only two days—no cuts, bruises or loss of sight. I was really amazed that his eye wasn't even bloodshot.

I hired a private investigator after we had been dating for a year and these crazy episodes continued. He told me that Michael was divorced (something I didn't know) and that a girlfriend had once pressed charges for theft.

It turns out Michael hadn't told me the truth about anything. He promised me the world, but he turned out to be just a jerk.

David's Grand Fabrication

Two and a half years ago, I moved from Texas to Colorado to start a new job. My grandparents lived there, so I had family close by. I met David soon after I arrived. He impressed me instantly with his charm and self-assurance. He was one of the smartest men I had ever met, so I wasn't surprised to find out he

•

was going to law school. In Texas, I had been involved with a series of losers, so I was thrilled to finally meet someone who had a professional career ahead of him.

After we had been dating for six months, David moved in with me. Soon after that, I discovered I was pregnant. We had already been talking about marriage so we decided the time was right. My grandparents helped me plan the wedding, and they covered most of the expenses. David told me his family would pay for the honeymoon. We planned to go to Florida over the Thanksgiving holiday.

But the day before our wedding, David told me his parents hadn't yet come through with the honeymoon cash, so I ended up writing checks to cover the airfare and hotel. I was angry at David's parents, but he assured me I would be reimbursed. It was not until much later that I learned his parents had never promised to pay for anything.

In January I called David's law school to find out what we owed for tuition. I was really shocked when they told me they had no record of my husband's ever being enrolled in their school. In fact, he had never even received an undergraduate degree. When I confronted David, he admitted he wasn't officially en-

•

rolled but had been auditing classes at the law school. I was speechless. We had a baby on the way, and my husband wasn't even close to finishing college, much less getting a law degree.

I was still trying to digest all this new information when a man came to our door. He said he represented a car-rental agency in Missouri, and they believed our car had been stolen from them. He was very reasonable. He said if we gave the car back, the agency would not press charges. After he left, I went into the bathroom and vomited. Then I packed David's bags. When he came home, his things were sitting on the front porch. I told him to get out, and my grandfather helped me find a lawyer to arrange the divorce.

In May I gave birth to a beautiful baby girl. David has never made any effort to see her, and I'm relieved about that. Maybe I'll never have to tell her the real truth about her father.

Words cannot describe how traumatized I was by this whole mess. I always thought I was such a good judge of character. I realize if this could happen to me, it could happen to any woman.

The sad refrain of women who have been conned is, "I don't know if I'll ever trust a man again." A Con

•

Carol Rosen

Man will rob you of more than your money and time. He'll rob you of your belief in the goodness of people. That's the real damage. Marsha's case is particularly horrifying. She did find a decent man—but only after she paid (and is still paying) a high price for her first marriage.

Marsha and the Swindler

My husband, Frederick, was the owner of a multimillion-dollar manufacturing firm. Things were going so well that shortly after we were married, he came home and announced, "Business is so terrific that I'm putting a subsidiary in your name." I was very excited about this, and I signed the papers without thinking twice about it. We really had the good life—but things were not as they seemed.

One day Frederick came home early and told me to straighten the house because the bank was coming to take a look at it. What he didn't mention was that the bank was bringing federal agents. To my complete shock, they announced they were confiscating everything—the house, the cars and all we owned. Plus, they were freezing all our assets.

Slowly, the story came out. Federick was a

•

70

compulsive gambler—something I had been completely unaware of—and he'd been having serious cash-flow problems. He'd gambled away his company's assets and was delinquent in paying his taxes. When he realized he was in deep trouble, he had me sign those papers. They were not for a subsidiary, as he had told me. They were for his company. Suddenly, I had complete legal and financial responsibility for the mess he'd created.

He owed the federal government two hundred fifty thousand dollars—and he owed everyone else, too. My life was a nightmare for years because of this, and we eventually divorced.

At first I thought I would *never* be able to trust another man, but I lucked out. I met and married my current husband, who knew all along about my financial status. Together, we are still paying off Frederick's debts while Frederick is living with his *second* wife. Guess whose name his new business is in?

•

Chapter Four
·
The Sleazy
Lover

*He's "God's Gift to
Women"*

 T he Sleazy Lover thinks he's so irresistible to women he can't help being unfaithful. Even if he swears he loves only you, he's always got this eyes peeled, looking for his next conquest. He claims to love women, but it's not love; it's a form of sexual control.

Joan called the Jerkline to tell me about her experience with Lou, the man she'd divorced that year. They had been married for eight years when she found out he was "dating" high-class call girls.

·

"I was shocked," Joan told me. "I mean, having an affair is one thing, but *call girls*? And you won't believe the reason he gave. He said, 'They're so intelligent. They have master's degrees.' I would have laughed, but it hurt too much."

Sleazy Lovers have inflated opinions of their sexual prowess. They'll tell you, "No man has ever pleased you the way I can," or say, "You've never been with a real man." Their come-ons are beyond belief. One woman told me about a man who said, moments after they met, "I have an overwhelming urge to cuddle in your cleavage." Men like this think they're being sexy and cute, but most women recognize these pickup lines for what they are: sleaze.

And let's face it: Sometimes these guys are all talk and no action. Lynn called the Jerkline to tell about a man like that:

The Fizzled Lover

This man was courting me like gangbusters. He insinuated that he was a very virile lover, with great sexual prowess. He'd invite you out, and you'd know right away that there would be no dinner, no show, no party. He had only one thing on his fevered little mind: *sex.*

Well, after weeks of listening to his advertising, I finally decided to give him a try.

•

[Isn't that the American way—try it and buy it?] But when I finally went to bed with him, he couldn't perform. I almost had to laugh. This guy was good for nothing. And I mean *nothing.*

Men have been having affairs since the beginning of time. I think the only man who was completely exempt was Adam, and that's just because there were no other women around. The man who has affairs is a champion liar. Sometimes he'll keep lying even after he's been caught. Here's an example of one of the most amazing lies I heard:

Peace Corps Romeo

I believe my ex-boyfriend is a little warped. He was a Peace Corps volunteer in Guatemala, and when I visited him there, I discovered he had not only befriended several other women, he'd slept with them, too. I was upset, but he later defended his actions in a letter, hoping to clarify the situation. He wrote that when he was with others, "It was just a release of tension. . . . I thought of you and even called out your name. . . . It was you I wanted to be with, and it was you I fantasized about. . . .

•

Honey, for all practical purposes, it was you
I made love to."

This was the creepiest line I ever heard.
Needless to say, that was the end of our relationship.

Many women wrote and called to tell me of men
who cheated on them right from the start of the
relationship and kept on lying about it, even when
the evidence was irrefutable. Here's one story:

The Lying Lover

I met Stuart ten years ago, when I was thirty
and he was twenty. He cheated, lied and manipulated me from the first day we met. Even
though I knew he cheated on me and lied
about seeing other women, I still forgave him
in my heart.

We broke up one and a half years ago, when
I had finally had enough of his behavior. To
this day, Stuart has never been truthful and
admitted he saw other women. But his behavior hasn't changed. He's now living with
the second woman he's been with in the last
year, and he still comes around to my house.
He's always saying he loves me and wants me
back. He'll tell me things like, "Oh honey,

●

Diane's on her way out. All you have to do is give me the word." Over my dead body! I happen to know he's cheating on Diane with at least two other women. Some things never change.

Because Sleazy Lovers only care about themselves and are overly focused on sex, they will leave women if things don't go just the way they want them to. I've heard many stories of Sleazy Lovers who walked away or found other women just when their wives or girlfriends needed them most. Compassion and true supportive love are not their strong suits. To paraphrase an old saying: When the going gets tough, the Sleazy Lover gets going.

I found some of these stories heartbreaking.

Trust Betrayed

We had been married for thirty-four years when my husband started having an affair with a friend of mine who lived right around the corner. What really broke my heart was that he started the affair while I was in the hospital and continued it while I recovered. I was in a wheelchair for a while and had to use a walker for almost a year. He was seeing

•

her all that time. And she was supposed to be my friend!

Finally, just when I was starting to get better, he asked me for a divorce. He left me and moved in with her.

I was completely flabbergasted. I really learned a lot about trust. My husband was the kind of person you'd never suspect of this kind of thing. He was a deacon in our church for twenty years and had never given me reason to doubt him. I guess it's true that there's no fool like an old fool. Now I wonder if my friend was the first woman, or if he'd been lying to me all along.

Hit and Run Scott

Scott and I lived together for three years. We were about to be married when I became seriously ill with uterine cancer. It was terribly stressful for both of us. I was in the hospital numerous times for surgery and radiation treatments. I'd love to tell you what a stand-up guy Scott was, but most of the time I had to cheer *him* up, not the other way around. I was very sick and terribly weak, and he complained constantly that the stress of my illness

•

78

was getting to him. I couldn't keep his spirits up after a while, never mind my own.

During this period, Scott lost his job and he decided to move to California to find work. This was two weeks before I was scheduled for major surgery. He suggested I could move in with my parents until I got better, then join him in California. That's what I did. But when I finally recovered and was ready to move, he announced he didn't want me anymore. He was living with another woman in California. He told me since I couldn't have children now, I wasn't the woman for him. You can imagine how this made me feel. I had wanted children, too.

The real joke is that all this was from a man who never even made support payments for the children he had from his first marriage.

Deserters are a particularly vicious breed of Sleazy Lover. The worst thing about Deserters is that when they walk away from marriages, they often leave their wives and children in very bad economic circumstances. According to research by Lenore Weitzman, associate professor of sociology at Stanford University, the effect of the average divorce decree is to decrease the standard of living of a woman and her children by 73 percent, while actually increasing the man's by

•

42 percent. And that doesn't even take into account the emotional damage done to the children of divorce or the now-single mother who must restore her children's sense of security while trying to maintain her own stability. The woman who related the following story wondered how she would ever explain to her children why their father left them.

Husband on the Lam

Four years ago, my husband, Mark, lost his job and decided he needed to go to Arizona, where his family lived, to look for work. We had two children, a two-year-old son and a four-year-old daughter who had rheumatoid arthritis and needed lots of care.

I was worried, because Mark had an old car, and I wasn't sure it could make the trip. But he told me not to worry and said he loved me and the kids more than anything, and soon we'd all be together. He made a big point of saying he was doing this for us.

A week went by without a word from him, and I was worried sick. I called his family in Arizona, but they hadn't heard from him. I contacted a friend of mine who was with the local police, and he told me to wait another week. I did, and when there was still no word,

•

my friend put out an all-points bulletin on him. I was frantic. I knew something terrible had happened.

Three days after I filed the missing person's report, Mark called my office shortly before I arrived at work. He told my boss he was in Nevada, working at a gas station because he'd thrown a rod in his car. He told my boss to tell me he was fine and would be in touch.

I thought the whole thing was very weird. Now that I knew he was okay, it didn't make any sense that he wasn't in touch. He could have called me at home. The more I thought about it, the more suspicious I got.

I got in my car and drove to the house of his former girlfriend, and sure enough, there he was. He had never even left town. We had all worried for nothing.

Sleazy Lovers never take responsibility for their actions. For them, sex is just a game they play: spill your seed and walk away. They seldom view women as real. As one man told his girlfriend when she complained about the way he was treating her, "A woman is just a life-support system for a vagina."

That's pretty much the way the man in this story felt.

•

Dean's Escape

Jerk men are the story of my life. Among the worst was Dean, the man I was dating right after I graduated from college. We had been going steady for six months, but I hadn't slept with him because I believed it was important to stay a virgin until marriage. But one night he got drunk at a party and forced me to have sex with him. Once it was over, Dean held me in his arms and told me it was all right because he loved me and we would be together forever.

But the next week, Dean announced he was moving from California to the East Coast. He promised to send for me soon. I really believed he wanted me and that someday we would be together. Then I found out I was pregnant. I called and told him, but Dean refused to have anything more to do with me. He didn't really want me, after all. I had to go into hiding because my family would have died if they'd known I got pregnant outside of marriage. The whole experience was horrible. I went through it alone and gave the baby up for adoption.

I never heard from Dean again.

The Sleazy Lover is so unaware of how despicable and disgusting his actions are that he'll stop at noth-

•

ing. One woman told me on the Jerkline that after her husband had moved out to live with his mistress, he called her to complain about the size of the woman's bed. "He wondered if he could come over and exchange beds, because I didn't need our king size anymore and they did!"

Another woman told me how her husband wanted to stay married to her and also keep his mistress. When she said, "You want to have your cake and eat it, too," he gave an answer that perfectly sums up the philosophy of Sleazy Lovers: "I like cake."

That's the whole point with Sleazy Lovers: They like "cake," and lots of it. The following letters are typical of those I received from women who were heartbroken by the actions of men who promised them true love but played around on them. It might seem easy to say, "Hey, you should have dumped this jerk." But these women really loved and trusted their men. Even when they caught them in the act, they believed the men when they promised it would never happen again. Of course, it always did.

Infidelity in the Military

I'm in the navy. While I was stationed in the Philippines, I met and started dating Carl, another navy guy. We dated for two years, and he was a jerk. I'm almost ashamed to say I

•

stuck with this guy, but it's hard to find a date in a place like the Philippines.

I ignored the early signs that this wasn't a decent guy. One night at the beginning of our relationship, he called me to cancel a date, claiming he was sick. I didn't think anything of it, but later in the week my best friend told me she heard that Carl was out with another woman Friday night, and they were seen behaving very affectionately.

Well, after I went ballistic and took him to task, Carl apologized and promised never to lie to me again. After that, things seemed to get better. But about seven months after this incident, Carl broke a date with me because he said a friend had come in on temporary duty, and Carl and another guy were going to take him out and show him a good time. I thought nothing of it until a few days later when someone asked me if Carl and I were having problems. When I asked why, he got uncomfortable, then admitted he'd seen Carl out with a woman—the very night he was supposed to be out with the guys. I was very hurt, and when I confronted Carl, he admitted it and said she was the old friend who had come in on temporary duty. He said he didn't feel he could tell me his old friend was a

•

woman, and besides, he assured me he hadn't slept with her or anything.

I ended the relationship anyway. He kept begging me to take him back, and I finally did, because I really loved him. He even asked me to marry him. When we went to Hawaii on vacation, he chose a very romantic setting where he gave me a ring.

But after we became engaged, he got very moody and depressed. He kept talking about how he needed more space. He accused me of clinging to him and being possessive. I tried really hard to change my behavior and give him the space he said he needed.

Everything came to a head one night when there was a party at the base. Carl said he didn't want to go and told me to go ahead anyway and have a good time. I did, but later I decided I wanted to be with Carl, and I went over to his place. I had a key to his house, so I let myself in. He met me on the landing, looking like he'd just awakened. He seemed alarmed and pulled me into the living room. He was acting very strange, and suddenly I got the idea he wasn't alone. I ran to the bedroom, and sure enough, there was a woman in his bed. I went berserk.

It turns out Carl had been dating her for

•

several weeks, even though I was wearing his engagement ring. That was it for me—finally. I can't believe it took so long for me to wake up to the fact that one woman was never going to be enough for Carl.

Most Sleazy Lovers try to hide their extracurricular activities from you, but some of these guys are so sleazy, they can't seem to help themselves. They'll hit on your girlfriends right in front of you. It doesn't seem possible, but as the following two stories reveal, it happens.

The Double-Crosser

I met Paul at a hotel bar one night when my friend Judy and I were out on the town. He was with a friend, and they seemed like nice guys, so we hung out with them. Sparks really flew between me and Paul, and before the evening was over, he asked me for a date.

After only two dates, he told me he was falling in love with me. I was bowled over, because I had never seen a man get serious so fast. Usually, it was the other way around.

We went together for several weeks, and things got more and more intense. Then the bombshell came. Judy visited me one night,

•

and I could see she was very nervous and upset. I asked her what was wrong, and she said, "I hate to tell you this, and I hope you don't despise me, but I care too much for you to keep the truth from you."

Then she showed me several letters, and told me Paul had written them to her. I could hardly stand to read them. He wrote how attracted he was to her, and that he was infatuated by her beauty. He also wrote that he liked me but didn't think we were right for each other. He was ready to dump me if Judy wanted him.

I was hurt and angry and started to cry. This seemed too cruel for words. Today, when I look back on it, I'm grateful Judy was honest with me. At the time, however, I was too crushed by Paul's lies to think straight. I took my phone off the hook and cried for days. When I was finally ready to talk to Paul, I called him every name in the book. Neither Judy nor I have heard from him since. As the saying goes, good riddance to bad rubbish.

Jack's Libido

I lived with the world's biggest jerk for ten years. I never really admitted it until after I

•

left him, because I was too embarrassed. The clincher came when he went after my best girlfriend, practically right in front of me.

Jack and a friend had been out drinking that night, as usual. (Getting drunk and looking at naked women were Jack's favorite pastimes.) My girlfriend was visiting me and we were both asleep when Jack came home. She was sleeping on the couch. He went over and started kissing her and telling her how much he wanted her. She pushed him off, but he kept coming back and bothering her. All this was happening while I was asleep in the other room. My girlfriend finally came into my bedroom and slept with me for the rest of the night for protection.

Maybe you could make excuses for him by saying he was drunk, but since this was pretty typical behavior, I decided I didn't need the abuse anymore. So I left him.

It's not always so easy to leave, however, especially if you're married to a Sleazy Lover. Most people take their marriage vows seriously, but he sees them as a way of making sure you stay home waiting for him while he spreads his bounty elsewhere. These two stories make that point.

•

The Two-Woman Man

I was Greg's fourth wife, but he assured me I was different from all the rest, that finally he had found someone he really loved. In the first months of our marriage, it was heavenly. He was so supportive and loving. We bought a new house, and he promised that the past was really over.

But one night, after we had been married nearly a year, he exploded and said, "I've been dying to go out with other women!"

That wasn't quite true, it turned out. He'd already *been* going out with other women the entire time we'd been married. I should have known, but I was so in love with him I was blind. He had me completely fooled.

Wandering Walt

I was married to Walt for eight years and worked to support him while he attended police academy. When he started working, I quit my job, and we had a beautiful baby boy. Everything was perfect the first three years of our marriage. I was ecstatically happy.

Then Walt started doing a disappearing act.

•

He would tell me he was meeting his friend Mark for coffee and be gone for hours. He'd come home with a hickey on his neck after he had supposedly been playing cards with the boys. I tried to ignore it, hoping he'd settle down. I put all my energy into making our home life wonderful for him. But he kept it up, and finally the evidence was too over-whelming. He didn't even seem to care if I found lipstick on his shirts or receipts for gifts he had given someone else.

I sat Walt down and told him what I suspected. To my amazement, he admitted everything. Then he said, "I'm glad you brought it up because I've been meaning to talk to you. I've fallen in love with someone else, and I want a divorce. Jeanne and I are moving in together."

Carol, I should have left him in the beginning, but I believe if you're married you have an obligation to make things work out. Unfortunately, Walt didn't feel the same way. Now I'm alone, and I don't know if the wounds will ever heal.

The Sleazy Lover wants every woman to think he's interested only in her. And he is, as long as you don't

•

give him everything he wants. But once you do, it is only a matter of time before he moves on. It's not unusual for him to deny he ever had feelings for you. One woman told me how her lover of six years said, before he moved out, "I never loved you. I don't even *like* you." Can you imagine someone being so cruel? The following story is another tale of false love:

Tina's First Love

Tina called the Jerkline to tell me about Dan, her first love and the man who took her virginity. "I was crazy about him," she said sadly, "but as soon as he got what he wanted—sex—he started to sleep around. He even moved back in with his old girlfriend and told me it was just platonic. He said he was living with her for financial reasons. I was young, naïve and deeply in love, so I believed him."

Tina's voice shook with emotion when she told me what happened next:

> Soon I couldn't deny the truth anymore, because Dan got his old girlfriend pregnant. He married her, and I tried to go on with my life, even though I was completely shattered. Sometimes he'd call me and tell me he still loved me, and it was very tempting for me.

•

When you feel so much love for a person, it's hard to stop wanting them. Also, there is a special bond with the first person you make love to. That night meant so much to me, but I now see it meant nothing to him. It makes me very sad that someone can be that cold.

Sometimes, with a Sleazy Lover, revenge can be sweet. That was Sandy's story when she called the Jerkline. A bright and articulate woman, she got mixed up with a scheming liar. Sandy told me she met Matt when she was home visiting on a vacation from college. He said he was in the process of breaking up with his girlfriend, and after he met Sandy, he did.

After she returned to college, Sandy and Matt maintained a close relationship. He would visit her, or she would visit him, every weekend. Then Matt met a woman named Lisa, and he told Sandy about her. He liked Lisa, but only as a friend. He insisted the relationship was platonic, and Sandy believed him. As she told me, "I'm a modern woman. I have male friends, and I saw no reason why Matt shouldn't have platonic female friends."

Then one day Sandy was in town unexpectedly, and she decided to pay Matt a surprise visit; she was the one surprised. As she was entering the building where

•

Matt lived, another woman was leaving. Sandy immediately recognized her; they were old friends.

"Lisa!" she cried. "What are you doing here?"

"Sandy!" Lisa was just as surprised to see her old friend. She explained, "I was just checking up on my boyfriend. I was worried about him because he stood me up for a date last night, and that's not like Matt."

"Matt?" Sandy asked, as her heart sank. She could tell that her friend had no idea about Sandy's relationship with Matt, so she suggested they go into his apartment and talk.

It turned out that Matt and Lisa had been going out for two months. Matt had never mentioned Sandy, even though he'd said to her just the week before, "You're the only one I want to be with. I love you." Lisa admitted to Sandy that she and Matt had slept together on their first date.

By the time the two women had compared notes, both were ready to kill Matt. "Where is he?" growled Lisa. "I want to get my hands on that bum."

"I don't know," said Sandy, "but let's wait for him."

At last Matt returned home. As Sandy told me, "Carol, he turned white and started shaking when he saw us. I thought he was going to have a heart attack and die right there."

After telling Matt exactly what they thought of him,

•

Carol Rosen

the two women left. They remained friends, but Matt was out in the cold.

"It felt great!" Sandy admitted.

Another story of revenge came from a man who called the Jerkline and said, "I just have to tell you what my little sister, who's five feet two and weighs one hundred pounds soaking wet, did to her six-foot-two, two-hundred-pound husband."

I was intrigued. "What did she do?"

He laughed and told the following story:

> My little sister always had a bad temper, but I didn't know what she was capable of. Her husband was cheating on her, and the whole family knew about it. We tried to tell her, but she wouldn't believe us. She'd say, "Not my husband." But then the other woman called her up and told her everything, and she flew into a rage.
>
> There were four of us there when she stormed into the house. Her husband was taking a shower. She went straight into the bathroom, and suddenly we heard him screaming bloody murder. We ran in. My little sister had dragged him out of the shower by the balls, and she wouldn't let go. He was begging and

•

94

crying and practically passing out, but she was screaming, "They're coming off! They're coming off!' She held on for seven minutes. She's just a little wisp of a girl. None of us could believe it, especially him. I'll tell you one thing—her husband has never cheated again.

•

say the words 'I love you.' I wanted him to say them, but I figured that actions speak louder than words.

"Eric was afraid of commitment. I knew that from the start. I wasn't in any rush myself, and I let him know I was willing to take it slow and easy and give him all the time he needed. But the years went by, and he showed no signs of getting more serious.

"Finally, two weeks ago, I decided to say something. We had been dating for six years, and had spent every holiday, vacation and several evenings a week together. All our friends considered us a couple. I didn't think I was jumping the gun. So I said, very gently, 'Eric, I love you, and I know you love me. Maybe it's time we started thinking about making a commitment.' "

She paused to compose herself. "Carol, I wasn't giving him an ultimatum. I wasn't saying, 'Marry me now or else.' I was just suggesting that we start *talking* about it."

"How did he respond?" I asked.

"It was horrible. I couldn't believe his reaction. He got very agitated, then he said, 'I don't know what I want from this relationship.' I'm afraid I lost it. I started crying and screaming, 'You don't know after six years?' He stayed very calm. He said, 'I'm sorry. I'm not ready to have this conversation. But it obviously means a lot to you, so maybe we should see less of each other for a while.'

•

"Carol, I was so shocked and hurt. I stormed out, and I haven't spoken to him since. But I can't stop crying. I don't know what to do."

There wasn't much I could say to her. I didn't think she was ready to hear the truth: Eric was a Charming Scoundrel who would probably never be ready to make a commitment. She had devoted six years of her life to a man she believed was Mr. Right—and he wasn't having any of it.

It's hard to imagine the pain this realization brings, and few women who are with Charming Scoundrels are ready to hear the truth when it comes. Eric is a classic example. He'd rather walk away after six years than even *discuss* the future.

Charming Scoundrels will leave you in limbo, sometimes for years. And they always have plenty of excuses. Here are just a few of the ones I heard:

"You're too good for me."

"I don't know what I want."

"I like things the way they are."

"I've been hurt too much in the past."

"I can't settle down until I have more money."

"I've never seen a happily married couple."

"When I'm ready, you'll be the one."

"I need to find myself."

"I never said 'I love you.' "

The list goes on and on. You invest all your energy

•

and emotions in a relationship that comes to a dead end. It's not fair, and a Charming Scoundrel isn't always easy to spot. He may be the perfect boyfriend in every way. Like Helen, you might not have a clue until you're deeply into the relationship that there's no future in it.

No matter what excuse he offers, the result is the same: You're left in limbo. If you have dreams of marriage and children, you can forget them. He may be very good at implying potential commitment, but most Charming Scoundrels have no intention of ever marrying.

You may decide to remain in the relationship, believing you are the one who can make him change, that once he sees how much you love him, his fears will melt away and he'll beg you to marry him. The sad truth is, you cannot change anyone except yourself.

Charming Scoundrels can give you a real roller-coaster ride. They've been known to go from desperately wanting a commitment to grabbing their track shoes and running off within weeks. That was Stacy's experience:

Stacy's Flash-in-the-Pan

I met Frank in a bar, and we hit it off. Our first date was a lot of fun—dinner, a show,

•

the "works"—and he didn't try to get me into bed. He kissed me good night and said, "Let's save the other stuff for later."

Frank called me three times the following week, and we talked for hours. We had so much to talk about that the time just flew by. During one of these conversations, Frank shocked me by saying, "Let me ask you a hypothetical question: If I were to ask you to marry me, would you?" I was bowled over. "We've only known each other two weeks!" I said. But he seemed serious and kept pressing me for an answer. I was beginning to think maybe there's such a thing as love at first sight. Finally, I said, "If the time comes, okay, but we really need to get to know each other better." He told me to keep it in mind, and we made a date for the following Saturday night.

On our second date, things got strange. Frank seemed distant and cool, and he whisked me home after dinner. I asked him what was wrong, and he said, "I feel uncomfortable—like you want to rush me into marriage."

I was shocked and embarrassed. "I'm not rushing you into anything!" I said. *"You're* the one who mentioned marriage. This is ab-

•

solutely ridiculous." But that was it. I never
heard from Frank again.

Some Charming Scoundrels are in love with the
idea of falling in love—or, rather, making you fall in
love with them. They thrill to the chase, but once you
surrender, they aren't interested anymore. Here are
two stories of men who swept women off their feet,
then dumped them in a heap:

Gene's Empty Pursuit

I met Gene and he began to pursue me. We
worked in the same office, and we'd see each
other in the elevators. He'd always start a conversation with me. At first I wasn't interested,
but he was persistent. We started dating two
or three times a month, and he told me I was
an angel from head to toe. Two months ago,
I had an operation to remove a benign tumor,
and Gene came to the hospital with flowers.
He said he could hardly wait to see me again
when I felt better. He called me every day
while I was recovering.

The day I returned to work, Gene buzzed
me on the intercom and asked me to come
into his office. I was surprised because we had

•

been trying to keep our relationship a secret at work. He told me he was happy to see me back, and we made a date for the following Friday night.

On that date, I stayed over at his apartment for the first time. It was a wonderful night, but the next morning he started to find fault with me. I felt like I was getting on his nerves. Then he didn't call me the following week. When I saw him at work, he gave me an abrupt excuse about being busy. His behavior really upset me, and I started brooding about it. Finally, I got up my courage and called him at home to ask why he was avoiding me. He put me off, saying he couldn't talk then. A few more days went by without a word from him.

Finally, Gene called and said, "I really like you, but I have to be honest. I just don't have time for a relationship right now." I was upset and started to cry. "You told me you loved me," I said. He replied, "I love you but I'm not *in* love with you."

That was the end of our relationship. And even though we still work in the same office, I rarely run into him anymore. He got off scot-free, but the experience left me a basket case for months.

•

The relationship described in the next story was even shorter:

The Bum's Rush

This guy lavished attention on me for five weeks—flowers, dinners, phone calls, romantic evenings and fabulous sex. He made me feel like the heroine of a romance novel. Then suddenly it stopped. His reason? "I don't love you, I don't want to marry you, so I can't see you anymore." Our relationship was shorter than the Gulf War. We met one week before it started and broke up one week before it ended. He launched his missiles, devastated me and walked away.

The Charming Scoundrel is an expert at slipping away. The last thing he wants is a personal confrontation. Once he decides it's time to move on, he just stops calling you, or avoids seeing you. You might date this man for years, only to have your relationship abruptly terminated. The man in the following story couldn't even show his girlfriend the courtesy of a face-to-face breakup:

•

The Cowardly Kiss-off

After a wonderful relationship of two and a
half years, my boyfriend wrote me a letter
saying, "This may come as a shock to you,
but I feel I have to be honest. We're too different to stay together. I love you and respect
you as a friend, but I'm not *in* love with you,
and I think it would be best if we stopped
seeing each other romantically."

The wimp had the nerve to send me a letter!
He couldn't even tell me to my face. And he
couldn't stop at just ending the relationship.
He had to insult me in the process. He wrote,
"I want someone who's more intelligent, mo-
tivated, sociable and involved." I didn't know
whether to laugh or cry. I was just so hurt.
This is the coldest move I've ever seen.

The worst type of Charming Scoundrel is the man
who is still attached to the past. He may tell you he's
been so hurt that he's afraid to get involved. Or he
may still be emotionally tied to a woman he loved before he met you. Either way, he's not going to be emotionally available to you. When a man says, "I can't
commit because I've been too hurt," you should run
like crazy. That's what this woman should have done:

•

Carol Rosen

The Wounded Boy

When Vinnie said, "I want to take things slow because my ex-wife really messed me up, and I'm afraid of being hurt," I should have said, "You don't have to worry about me hurting you. I'm out of here!" But instead, I sympathized with him and decided he was worth waiting for, even if it took time. I was the first woman he'd been with since his divorce—or that's what he claimed.

Well, he led me on. We dated for five months, and things went nowhere. My friends were all urging me to give it up, but I stayed. He's the one who left. He told me he needed a few weeks to clear his head. Well, a few weeks became a month, then two months. You know the rest of the story. That was two years ago, and I haven't heard from him since.

The next letter is from a woman who lived with the ghost of her boyfriend's former love:

The Package Deal

I met Chuck in September 1989. We fell in love and moved in together after four months. I was thrilled because I believed Chuck was

•

the man for me. But as soon as we moved in together, he started bringing up Candi, his ex-girlfriend. He mentioned her so much it was as if she were an invisible partner in our relationship. For example, after dinner one night, Chuck let out a big sigh. I asked him what was wrong, and he said, "The spaghetti was good, but it made me think of Candi's wonderful homemade sauce." I was insulted, but I let that one go. Unfortunately, things grew progressively worse. When I wanted to see an old Bette Davis movie, Chuck said, "No, we can't rent that. It'll remind me of Candi." Then there was the time I commented on a bright red Firebird in the parking lot, and Chuck said sadly, "Candi always loved Firebirds." It got to the point where he even compared my lovemaking to Candi's. That was the last straw. I screamed, "If she was so great, why don't you go back to her?" That was the end for us.

One of the worst things a Charming Scoundrel can do is to actually set a wedding date and go through all the preparations with you, only to back out at the last minute. Here's what happened to one woman:

•

Carol Rosen

Wedding in Limbo

My girlfriend and I took a vacation to Maine.
The company I worked for had a plant there,
which we visited. Doug, the plant manager,
and I hit it off immediately. We carried on a
long-distance romance for seven months,
flying back and forth to see each other and
talking on the phone every night. Doug asked
me to marry him one night on the phone. I
accepted, and after many hours of discussion,
we agreed I should move to Maine, find a job
and a house and then we'd set a wedding date.
Since my company had a policy against married couples working together, I would have
to give up my seniority and find a job with a
new company, but I was willing to make the
sacrifice because I loved Doug.

I left my job, home, family and friends and
moved to Maine. Once I was there, I found a
good job, got some leads on houses and
started trying to discuss wedding plans. But
every time I mentioned the wedding, we got
into a fight. One evening I was discussing
color schemes, and Doug started to argue with
me. I was beginning to wonder if he really
wanted to marry me, so I put my foot down.

•

I told him, "You have until Saturday to set a date for the wedding or I'm leaving."

On Saturday I had to broach the subject. He said, "I want to marry you, but I can't say when." I tried to be reasonable. I said, "Well, are we talking about this year?" He said, "I don't know." So I asked, "Next year?" He shrugged. Suddenly, I saw the truth. I could still be waiting for a wedding five years from now. It was hard to walk away, but I had to do it.

Some Charming Scoundrels want it both ways. They want you to be around, but they won't make the commitment. If you try to leave, they'll romance you until you weaken, even promising marriage to keep you in line. But in the end, nothing changes. That was this woman's plight:

Promises, Promises

After Adam and I had been living together for two years, I suggested it was time to talk about marriage. Adam answered, "Why ruin a perfect relationship?" I was furious, so I split and moved back in with my parents. I even went on a date with another man and tried to put

•

all thoughts of Adam behind me. But shortly after my date, Adam showed up on my doorstep with an engagement ring and said, "Come home with me now. I love you, and I want to get married." He swept me off my feet. I was overjoyed. I moved back, and we started premarital counseling at our church.

But then things came to a grinding halt. Adam wouldn't do anything that moved us closer to marriage unless I nagged him. He made it clear we were two separate entities, not a couple. When I asked him about getting joint checking and savings accounts, he said, "Your money is yours, and mine is mine." Now it's looking like maybe we'll never get married. I'm embarrassed to admit to my parents it's not working out, so I'm staying with Adam until I save enough money to get a place of my own. But then I'm leaving.

Some men think that as long as they don't say the words "I love you" or make a verbal commitment, they're home free. It doesn't matter if you've been with them for years. In their minds, *words* speak louder than *actions*. That's what Liz discovered:

•

Liz's Loser

I went out with this guy for two years. I was deeply in love, and I told him, "I want to get married and have children." He started acting like a prosecutor in a court of law: *"Prove* I said I loved you. When did I *guarantee* we'd get married? I never made any promises." Can you believe it?

It can be very satisfying when you call the Charming Scoundrel's bluff and walk away. These two stories made me stand up and cheer. The first was from a women who left her Scoundrel on the doorstep:

I was going out with a guy in college, and we had a passionate relationship. But he dumped me after our second year. His weak excuse was that I was too good for him. Six months after we broke up, he showed up at my door with tears in his eyes, telling me what a terrible mistake he had made. I wasn't the least bit moved. He begged me to come back, and I said, "Thanks but no thanks," and closed the door in his face. I had decided he was right: I *was* too good for him.

•

Carol Rosen

Another woman who called the Jerkline made a wonderful discovery after she had been jilted by her third jerk. She told me:

> I've been with three jerks, and they each had an excuse to leave. Jerk Number One left because he said I was "too dependent." Jerk Number Two left because he said I was "too independent." Jerk Number Three left because—you guessed it—I was "too dependent." After that, I took all my self-help books and started a bonfire. These men were the ones who were mixed up. I decided I'm fine just the way I am!

•

Chapter Six

·

The Married Seducer

He'll Never Belong to
You

*E*verything you've always heard about having an affair with a married man is true. It will disappoint you, break your heart and probably waste the best years of your life.

Here are several absolute truths about the Married Seducer:

- He'll tell you his wife doesn't understand him—only you do.
- He'll say he hasn't slept with his wife for

·

months or even years (although he won't
have a good explanation for how she got
pregnant during that time).
• He'll tell you he wishes desperately he had
met you ten, fifteen or twenty years ago.
• He'll complain endlessly about his wife
until you're sick of hearing her name.
• He'll swear undying love, and say that in
his heart (where it "really counts") he's
married to you.
• He'll flatter you by telling you how much
smarter, more exciting and sexier you are
than his wife.
• He'll promise that someday you'll be together—when the children are grown,
when the promotion comes through, when
his wife recovers from an illness, when he
has the nerve to confront her . . .

If you buy his line, this is what your life will be
like:

• You'll live a secret existence and never be
able to introduce the man you love to family or friends.
• You'll spend every holiday, summer vacation, birthday and most nights alone.
• If you get pregnant, you can count on rais-

•

ing the child alone, or being talked into an abortion.
- You won't be able to celebrate the important moments of his or your life together.
- Your meetings will always be rushed and involve sex more than conversation or companionship.
- You'll never be able to go out to a restaurant, see a movie or do anything "normal" couples do.
- If you live in a small town, attend the same church or work in the same company, you'll have to tolerate seeing him with his wife at public gatherings.
- You'll never be able to explain when family and friends ask why you haven't "found a nice man."
- If he finally gets a divorce, chances are he won't marry you.
- You'll spend a lot of time crying.

It's a plain fact that in a relationship with a Married Seducer, he holds all the cards and gets all the goodies. You get only fleeting moments of satisfaction. One woman told me how she used to cry for hours every time her lover left the apartment after their twice-weekly liaisons. That's a lot of crying time! Another woman said she got so sick of listening to her

•

lover complain about his wife she lashed out at him, "If you hate her so much, why are you still with her? What's wrong with you?" She told me he looked shocked by her outburst. "I don't think he really hates his wife," the woman confided. "He just tells me that because he thinks it will make me feel better. But I'm sick of his whining."

After listening to many stories about Married Seducers, I reached the conclusion that these men have some major brain cells missing. They just don't get it. Listen to this man, and see if you agree:

The Double Jerk

I didn't receive very many calls from men on the Jerkline, but this one is priceless. A jerk in the flesh!

He began by telling me what a rough day he'd had. "I've been called a jerk twice today by two different women," he complained. "I still don't understand what I did wrong. Maybe you can tell me."

"I'll try," I said. "What happened?"

"I've had a mistress for twelve years, and my wife even knows about her. You might say we've reached an accommodation. So, today my mistress asked, 'Why did you ever marry your wife?' I said, 'Because I wanted regular sex.' I was kind of kidding, although it was partly true. My mistress got angry and said, 'You're a real jerk.' Then she asked me to leave.

•

"When I got home, my wife was surprised to see me. She said, 'So, did she dump you?' I told her what I had said about marrying her for regular sex, and she said, 'You're a jerk! How could you tell her the only reason you married me was for regular sex!'

"Now both of them are mad at me, and I'm not sure why. I thought we had an arrangement, and suddenly I'm the bad guy."

I was at a loss to explain it to him. Some men think they're Yul Brynner in *The King and I,* the royal bee buzzing from flower to flower, bestowing the precious gift of themselves on their grateful subjects. This jerk just didn't get it. He's not only hurting his wife, but his girlfriend as well. No wonder they're both furious!

There are different types of Married Seducers: those who flaunt it and those who try to keep it secret for as long as they can. Here's a perfect example of the latter:

What a Surprise!

I had dated Alex a few years ago, but hadn't spoken to him since. I was pleased when he called me, as he had never been completely out of my thoughts. On the phone, Alex told me that he had been thinking about me, and asked if we could meet for lunch the following

•

day. I agreed, and I confess I was quite excited.

Lunch was long and pleasant. We connected right away, as though we'd only been apart for days rather than years. By the time we got up from the table, it was early evening. We decided to go back to my apartment.

Sex with Alex had always been glorious, but it wasn't so good this time. We were out of our clothes moments after we came through my door, and his hands left trails of fire all over me. I had never wanted a man as much as I wanted Alex at that moment. We fell onto the sofa, and I reached down to touch him only to find he wasn't excited. I couldn't believe it. I did everything I could to arouse him, all to no avail. But since we'd had a couple bottles of wine at lunch, I chalked it up to alcohol and nervousness and didn't think much of it. When he invited me to accompany him on a business trip to Missouri, I jumped at the chance. The trip was fun, but again, the sex was terrible. I could tell something was wrong, and I even asked him about it, but he said he was just stressed out from work.

A couple of days after we got back, I called Alex at home, just to talk. I felt comfortable doing that since it seemed we were seeing each other again. I was surprised when a soft-

•

spoken woman answered the phone. When I asked for Alex, she said he wasn't home. Then she said, "This is Alex's wife. Can I help you?"

His wife! I was flabbergasted. I made up a quick lie about being someone Alex worked with and asked her to have him call me. When I hung up the phone, my heart was pounding. I went from being shocked to being furious. I wanted an explanation. No—I *deserved* an explanation.

When Alex called me, he was practically whispering into the phone. He told me that he'd been forced to get married when he got this woman pregnant, but it wasn't a true love match. Not like us. I told him in no uncertain terms that he was a cheating scumbag, and there was no "us." At first I was sad to lose him and angry that he'd tried to use me. But later I was glad I hadn't become more deeply involved with such a pitiful fool. What a jerk!

The biggest shock for the woman who is involved with a married man comes when and if he actually gets a divorce. Suddenly, he's not so eager to be with the woman he cheated on his wife with. He wants his freedom. For the first time in years, he's allowed to play the field without guilt. While he was married, you may have considered his wife your enemy—the

•

person who was standing in the way of your happiness. Once the divorce comes through, you may discover the real enemy is your lover. This woman's letter gives a perfect example:

Lady-in-waiting

A number of years ago, I made the mistake of getting involved with a married man. I was thirty, and he was forty. He was very persistent, charming and, of course, an unhappy, misunderstood husband. He told me he was staying in the marriage only because he couldn't bear to leave his children while they were so young.

There was nothing new about his line, but I was very attracted to him, and our affair got quite intense. He was the best lover I'd ever had. Most women would kill to have such incredible sex even once in a lifetime. He rented a studio apartment where we could meet, took me on a wonderful trip to Mexico, and saw or spoke to me every day. He made many, many declarations of his love and assured me we would be together forever, once his children were older. I was madly in love with him and was willing to accept anything he told me.

•

About a year into our affair, his wife found out, and all hell broke loose. The next couple of years were rough, with him going back and forth between his family and me. He kept begging me to be patient and promising me everything would work out. He wrote me love letters, called me constantly, and came to see me as often as he could. Whenever we were together, the sparks flew, and the magic of our time together erased all my doubts.

The years went by, and I kept hanging in, although I desperately wanted to be married and have children of my own. Finally, after twelve years, he divorced his wife—but he didn't marry me. Suddenly, he stopped calling me every day, and we saw each other less often. I couldn't understand what had gone wrong. Then I discovered the truth. It turns out he had fallen in love with another woman, and she was the one he married. I felt so betrayed, but he told me, "You are too much like my first wife."

Carol, I just couldn't believe it. He had played me for a fool. Now I'm in my forties, and I wonder if I've missed my chance to have a normal family life with children. If I don't find a nice man soon, it will be too late. This

•

man stole something priceless from me, and I let him do it. I'm ashamed of myself and disgusted with him.

You have to realize, for the Married Seducer, the real thrill is found in the unusual, the exotic, the different. Once you have an ongoing relationship with him, he may view you the same way he views his wife: dull and predictable. This story is a perfect example of how the tables are turned on the faithful girlfriend:

Seduced and Abandoned

I am a divorcée. A married man living in my condominium complex pursued me for five years until finally I gave in. He made excuses to see me every day and bought me gifts. He really came on strong, and I was lonely. I hadn't been with a man in a long time, so I finally let him seduce me.

I knew that married men seldom leave their wives for their lovers, so I was bowled over when he announced he was getting a divorce to be with me. It was like a dream come true.

But only five weeks after the divorce was final, he told me he had changed his mind. It seems he'd fallen head over heels in love with another woman. He had the nerve to tell me

•

how wonderful their sex life was. I think he expected me to be understanding, but the only thing I understood was the man was a louse.

Then there's the man who keeps going back to his wife. She's his security blanket when things get tough in the cruel, hard world. The women in the following three stories found out the hard way that Married Seducers are likely to escape to the past when things get too real in the new relationship.

Herb's Cop-out

I dated Herb for a year while he was still married. He finally divorced his wife, but when I got pregnant, he went back to her. He insisted the baby wasn't his. I asked him who else he thought I had been sleeping with, and his response almost blew my socks off: "A woman who'd have an affair with a married man would sleep with anybody," he said. When I slammed the phone down, our relationship was over. I realized I didn't want to be the mother of this man's child. What if it looked like him? I had an abortion.

Now he's calling me again. Even though he's remarrying his ex-wife, he wonders if we

•

can continue our relationship on the side. Carol, can you guess what I told him?

Torn Between Two Lovers

When I met Fred, he was married, but we became good friends After his divorce a year later, we eased into a romantic relationship. It was wonderful, but we both agreed to take things slow. I knew I loved him, but I didn't admit it until he told me how he felt about me. We were so happy. Finally, Fred moved in with me and he gave me a beautiful engagement ring.

Everything was fine until Fred's ex-wife, Christine, started calling the house very late at night. He would have lengthy conversations with her, but he assured me he didn't want her back. His excuse was that they still had some things to work out. Then one night we were at a local club, and Christine was there, too. Fred spent a lot of time talking to her, and they looked pretty cozy. I tried to ignore them and have fun with friends, but the sight of them together, huddled in a corner of the bar, made me sick. I couldn't stand it anymore and left in a huff.

Fred didn't come home that night or most

•

of the next day. You can imagine how hysterical I became. During that time, I cried until there were no tears left. When he finally walked in, he looked solemn. I wanted to tear him apart, but the angrier I became, the calmer he grew. He told me he'd been doing a lot of thinking, and maybe we'd rushed into our relationship too fast. He said, "I've always been tied down, and I need some freedom now." When I protested, he said he'd discussed this with Christine, and she understood. Why couldn't I? That was like a slap in the face. He didn't care about me at all. I was the one who stuck it out with him through all of his traumas with Christine, and now he was holding her up as if she were a saint.

He moved out that day, and I didn't hear from him for several weeks. Later I learned that he and Christine had started dating again. I am completely traumatized by what Fred did, and I want to warn other women to stay away from married or formerly married men. They'll bring you nothing but trouble and pain. Believe me, I know.

•

Carol Rosen

Patrick's Panic

This creep Patrick moved in with me three years ago. After we had been living together for six months, he confessed he was married. I should have kicked him out then, but I was crazy about him. I also believed him when he told me he was in the process of getting a divorce from his wife, who lived in another state.

A year went by and there was still no divorce. Patrick kept making excuses. I got pregnant and had an abortion because that's what he wanted. A few months later, I got pregnant again, and this time he encouraged me to keep the baby. I was thrilled. To me, this meant he seriously loved me and was planning our future together.

When I was seven months pregnant, he said he had to go away on a business trip. That was the last time I ever saw him. A few days after he left, he sent me a letter (with no return address) saying he'd gone back to his wife. Needless to say, I was shocked and destroyed. Now I'm a single mother, and I don't even know where Patrick is so I can get his help with child support.

After three years, I thought I knew him,

•

and I still can't believe I was so badly deceived.
I can't even look at men now. I don't trust
my judgment, and I don't trust them.

The Married Seducer doesn't want a real relationship. He wants a fantasy. There's something so ap-
pealing about having a mistress—a woman on the
side whom he doesn't have to see every day. No bills,
no chores, no screaming children. Just candlelight
and romance. It's the perfect setup. Once the fantasy
crumbles and you start to have a real day-to-day relationship, he can't handle it. If you don't want to
spend your life pretending to be some guy's Barbie
doll, you have to wake up and say to yourself, "He's
just a jerk and not worth the effort."
   This was my favorite letter about a Married Seducer.
I think it says it all:

   I met this guy at a singles bar, and didn't
   find out for two months that he was married.
   When I learned the truth and asked him why
   he had kept such a big secret from me, he
   just shrugged and said, "Because I'm a shit."
   Isn't that the understatement of all time?

•

the saying goes, "tied to his mother's apron's strings," but that's not necessarily the case. The Mama's Boy may just be a spoiled brat who has always had everything handed to him on a silver platter. There might not even be a mother lurking in the picture—and that can be a problem, too. He's expecting *you* to be his mother.

However, most Mama's Boys have an unhealthy attachment to their families—one that precludes any serious adult relationship. "Blood is thicker than water" is their rallying cry. As one man said in a nasty exchange with his wife: "Father, mother, brothers and sisters can never be replaced, but you can always replace a wife."

At the very least, this is a childish attitude. At its worst, Mama's Boy behavior can drive you straight up the wall. If you're looking for a "normal," adult relationship, forget it. The real kicker about being with a Mama's Boy is that you're dealing with two jerks—him and *his mother.*

The worst kind of Mama's Boy is the literal kind— the man who will drop everything to do his mother's bidding. It doesn't matter what *you* want or need. It doesn't matter how unreasonable her demands. What she wants is what she gets. The following story is a typical fiasco with mother and son:

•

Vacation from Hell

I'd like to tell you about my recent—and I hope my last—jerk.

Forty-year-old Jordan suddenly changed our plans to go on a camping trip together when his mother decided to visit from the West Coast during the same month we'd planned to go camping. *He* decided we would go to Death Valley instead—*with* his mother—because she had always wanted to visit there. (I had been looking forward to our camping trip.) Then he arranged for the *three of us to share a room together,* plus he invited a male friend along at the last minute—to *also* share the room with us—*all without checking with me.* When I protested that he hadn't told me we would not have a room to ourselves, Jordan said I was being selfish and was only thinking of myself. (We were all going to split the cost of the room. His attitude was that I was lucky to be invited to go with them at all. When I reminded Jordan that it was *my* vacation, too, he said, "No, it isn't. It's mine and my mom's vacation. You're just coming along." I might as well have been a piece of luggage.

"We had driven to southern California in my car, and after visiting Death Valley, I

•

planned to drive home alone. Jordan and his
mother were going to rent a car and visit
friends for two or three weeks before return-
ing. Imagine my surprise when Jordan proposed that I fly home and leave my car for
their use so they would not have to rent a car.
I said I could not afford airfare and, besides,
I needed my car to commute to work. He
suggested I get a ride with a friend. Our relationship did *not* survive this vacation!

Here's a man who had no qualms at all about sacrificing the needs of his family to cater extravagantly
to his mother:

At Whose Expense?

I could never understand how my husband
worked two jobs and still didn't have enough
money to pay the bills. I had a job, too, and
we lived a very simple life. Where did all the
money go?

I finally found out. He was giving his
mother all the money from one paycheck, plus
stocking her refrigerator every week and taking her to lunch twice a week. I wouldn't
begrudge her the money if she needed it. But
his mother lived in a better house than ours,

•

which was fully paid for, and had a substantial income from her late husband's police pension. He was sacrificing our comfort and security to keep his mother living in a high style. It just wasn't fair!

In the worse-case scenario, the Mama's Boy brings his mother into your home, where she resumes her role as the matriarch of the family. That's what happened in this horror story:

The Bullying Matron

Keith's mother moved in when our son, Bobby, was born. She was supposedly there to help me out, but right away she took over. I felt like Bobby was more her baby than mine. For example, she criticized me for not breastfeeding, implying that I was depriving my son of something important. Sometimes, if I started to go into the baby's room, Keith's mother would chide me, "Don't disturb him. I just put him down to sleep." She refused to consider using a diaper service or even buying Pampers, saying, "My children all used cloth diapers, and I managed to wash them. So can you."

I was very weak during the first month after

•

Bobby was born, so I didn't protest. I just let her do her thing. But as I started to get stronger, I resented her intrusive presence. I didn't think it was so unreasonable to want to have my baby to myself. Besides, it's important for a baby to bond with his mother, and she wasn't giving me a chance.

One night almost two months after Bobby's birth, I sat Keith down in the bedroom and told him we had to talk. I tried to explain calmly how I felt, but he twisted everything around and accused me of being ungrateful for the help this wonderful woman was providing. After that conversation, I just didn't know what to do. Sometimes I'd fantasize about taking Bobby and running away.

It has now been nine months, and Keith's mother is still living with us. She shows no signs of leaving. In fact, she's encouraging me to return to work. She says, "Don't worry. I'll take care of Bobby." I feel like I'm missing out on what should be the most wonderful time in my life. I live in a house where my own husband conspires against me with his mother. I just don't know what to do.

And get this story! Talk about moving in on your territory:

•

Homeless for Christmas

My boyfriend and I lived in a very small apartment, with only one bedroom. Our first Christmas together, his mother, who lived in a retirement community in Arizona, announced she was coming to visit. I had never met her before, but I know she had a very domineering way with her children.

We decided to put her up in a hotel close by, but a week before she arrived, she called and said to my boyfriend, "How can you let your mother stay in a hotel at Christmas?" When he explained to her how small our apartment is, his mother replied, "Why can't *she* stay in a hotel?" I thought it was unbelievably nervy of her to suggest it. After all, the apartment was my home. But my boyfriend actually tried to talk me into it. "Please do it for the sake of peace," he said. I told him, "If I spend Christmas in a hotel, there won't be any peace." He finally called his mother and told her she would have to stay in a hotel, and she threw a fit and decided not to come at all. My boyfriend blamed me, and he sulked all during the holidays.

Maybe his mother got what she really wanted, since we broke up in January.

•

When a man is infatuated with his mother, you'll never measure up. It's even worse when his mother disapproves of you. And why shouldn't she? You're a threat to her number-one position in her son's life. Woe to the woman who tries to come between a Mama's Boy and his first love—as the following story demonstrates:

Not Good Enough

I was never good enough for James's mother. When she looked at me, I could almost feel her distaste. She had expected her precious boy to marry someone from his social circle, but instead he married me, a country girl from a middle-class family. I'd never been to college, or traveled to Europe or done any of the things people in James's circle do. I'm sure she thought I would bring James down.

During the first year we were married, James visited his mother every Saturday afternoon. I wasn't included on these visits, but I happen to know there were other guests—sometimes single women. I resented being treated like some despicable form of white trash, but I tolerated it because I loved James, and knew he loved me.

But things got more complicated when we

•

had our first child. Now James wanted to take the baby on his weekly visits but still leave me behind. I said, "Come on, James, isn't it about time we all grew up and accepted the fact that we're married? It hurts me that I am not included when you visit your mother. I swear, she's hoping you'll leave me for someone else." He didn't respond, so I pleaded, "If you really loved me, you'd stand up for me and force your mother to deal with me."

But he just wouldn't listen. He really believed his mother would never change, and it was more important that he have a pleasant visit with her. "She's old," he said. "Give her a break. She's not going to change, so why don't you accept it? If you make an issue, you'll just create more tension."

He made me feel unreasonable, petty and foolish. Of course, he was right. I just let it go. In my opinion, the old bag will live forever and bury us all, but I'm not going to let it bother me. Now my husband and son visit her every week, and I use that time to meet friends and enjoy myself. The way I see it, it's her loss, not mine.

Here's another letter from a woman whose fiancé's family drove them apart:

•

Carol Rosen

One Determined Mother!

I wouldn't believe this story myself if it hadn't happened to me. I met Pete in a bar while he was on vacation in Florida from Massachusetts. We hit it off, and he asked me out the next night. We saw each other every night during the time he was visiting. That started an intense long-distance relationship, with Pete flying to Florida or me flying to Massachusetts every two months or so. This went on for almost two years.

In that entire time, I never met Pete's family, and at first I didn't care. I wanted to spend what precious little time we had together. But when things started getting serious, I thought it was time. Pete agreed, but whenever we made plans to see them, they were out of town. It was beginning to seem more than coincidental that each time I visited, his parents would be unavailable. I mentioned this to Pete. He said, "Oh, you have to understand my family. My mother is a very domineering woman. She doesn't like the idea of her baby—me—getting married, and I guess she figures as long as she doesn't meet you, you don't exist." He laughed when he said it, but

•

I was very hurt. I *did* exist, whether his mother liked it or not!

Eventually, we got engaged, and I moved to Massachusetts, where—lucky me!—I finally met his mother. She obviously disliked me from the start and didn't even try to get to know me. For the most part, she ignored me and talked to Pete as if I weren't even in the room.

Then the phone calls started. If I answered the phone, she would hang up. We knew it was her, and Pete asked her why she wouldn't talk to me. She told him I was a slut and not worthy of him. For months she waged a fierce campaign to convince Pete not to marry me. She even called him at work and went on and on about what a mistake he was making. You can imagine how this made me feel—especially because he never told her off.

Then came the crushing blow. We'd been living together for seven months and were planning to be married in the spring. One night he came home and told me he wasn't so sure we should get married. I started crying hysterically. I felt as though I were trapped in a battle against forces too strong to defeat. His mother was winning, and I couldn't do anything about it.

•

When Pete saw how crushed I was, he melted. He held me in his arms, kissing me and assuring me that he wouldn't hurt me for all the money in the world. "I'm sorry I doubted," he said. "Of course we're getting married, sweetheart."

After that, we proceeded to make plans for the wedding and honeymoon. We even spent an entire evening writing our invitations together. It was a very sweet and romantic period. Sometimes I'd look up at Pete, and we'd smile at each other with such happiness and contentment. We were going to be together, and nothing could stop us.

Then one night, six weeks before the wedding, I returned from work to find a message on my answering machine. It was from Pete, telling me to call him at his mother's. That was strange, and when I called, he picked up the phone on the first ring. He told me to sit down. He had something very important to tell me. His mother had had some kind of severe anxiety attack earlier that day and was rushed to the hospital. She was home now, sedated and resting, and he was going to stay with her. I didn't really understand what an anxiety attack was, so I asked him if it was serious. "Of course it's serious," he replied.

•

"She couldn't breathe. I'm very worried about her, and my father is a basket case. I can't come home until I know she's okay."

He ended up staying at his parents' house for a week, and he only called me once a day for brief chats. The whole thing made me very suspicious, but I thought I was being paranoid until the day he walked in and told me we had to postpone the wedding. He explained that it was too stressful for his mother, and he couldn't afford to do anything that might set her off again. He said, "I could never forgive myself if I did anything to hurt her."

I was aching inside, but I tried to stay calm. "People get married all the time, and their parents learn to accept it," I said. "I'm sure things will improve once she knows me better. Please, Pete, don't do this." He shook his head and repeated, "I'm sorry, I just can't take the chance."

So Pete's mother had won, after all. I felt totally defeated. I also realized that if Pete really loved me, he would never do this. It was pointless to argue. I knew I had to make a decision, and I ended up making the hardest choice of my life. I was thirty-seven years old, and I knew if I wanted children, I would have to get married soon. This wasn't going to hap-

•

pen with Pete. I decided to leave him and move back to Florida.

Carol, I can talk about it calmly now, but it's impossible to describe what a horrible time that was for me. There were days when I didn't even see the point of getting out of bed. I was severely depressed and wondered if I would ever love another man. Pete's face haunted my dreams for almost a year. There must have been a dozen times when I nearly picked up the phone and begged him to take me back. Some inner strength always stopped me— thank God.

I finally started to heal after I began seeing a therapist. She was wonderful, and I believe that her understanding and support saved my life. She was the first person who ever told me it was okay to be selfish, to go after what I want. Now I have some hope that my life will go on. Thoughts of Pete are becoming less frequent. And I don't know and don't care what ever happened to his mother.

It's no surprise that most Mama's Boys are spoiled rotten. They're used to being taken care of, and even the simple courtesies don't occur to them. They live a "me, me, me" existence—as the following story attests:

•

All Take, No Give

We argued, as any couple will, but most of the arguments were about his mother. They lived together, about ninety miles from the city where I lived. She made things impossible for me, and to this day I don't understand why. I guess she was just a vicious, bitter old woman. The most obnoxious thing was the way she controlled the telephone. She would leave it off the hook for hours, making it impossible for me to reach him. Sometimes when she answered it and heard my voice, she'd hang up.

He told me he had to live with her since he had asthma, and only she could minister to him properly. I finally gave up trying to compete.

Oh, one more thing. It should have been a tip-off that this guy was a Mama's Boy when he refused to provide oral sex—although he insisted I perform it on him. It's a classic case of Mama's Boy behavior: all taking and no giving.

A Mama's Boy often expects you to fit an idealized model of the good wife and mother—as defined by his own mother. It doesn't matter that times have

•

changed. He expects things to be just as they were for him when he was growing up. What have become the "good old days" for him are your greatest burden. Listen to this woman:

An Old-fashioned Pain

When I met Rick, he told me he had always dreamed of marrying an "old-fashioned" woman. I used to kid him about it because I was the opposite of old-fashioned. I had a master's degree in finance, a high-paying job, and I was a card-carrying member of the feminist movement. When our relationship got serious, I thought Rick had learned to love and accept me for who I was, instead of carrying around this perfect Mom-and-apple-pie picture of the woman he wanted to marry.

After we moved in together, I saw I was wrong. He expected me to prepare dinner every night, do the dishes, handle the laundry, and do all the housecleaning. When I protested, he said his mother had no trouble handling everything. What was wrong with me? "Nothing is wrong with me, you stupid bastard," I said, "except that your mother didn't have a full-time job and I do." He shrugged

•

it off, saying, "Well, that will change after we're married."

I was speechless. We had never discussed this, and he knew I loved my career. Yet he expected me to quit and stay home after we were married? When I challenged him, he said, "I told you I wanted an old-fashioned woman. I assumed you were willing to change, since you let the relationship progress to this point." The rest of the story is obvious. We're no longer together. I assume he's out looking for that good "old-fashioned" woman. She can have him.

Watch out for the Mama's Boy who is used to being waited on hand and foot. Several women described men, well into their thirties or even forties, who had never had to take responsibility for paying their own bills, doing their laundry, cooking their meals or anything. These men often brag that they've arranged their lives perfectly. "I've got it made," one woman's boyfriend boasted. "Why should I want to change it?" This attitude signals a man whose emotional growth has been permanently stunted. The following letters tell the story:

•

Spoiled Rotten

I spoiled my boyfriend rotten. I was fifty, and he was thirty-six and still lived at home with his parents. He said he loved older women, and now I know why. This guy didn't work half the time. I worked hard, then cooked him wonderful meals. The only time he wanted sex was after he'd been drinking. If I didn't make a move on him, I wouldn't get sex.

He kept saying he was planning to move in with me, but there was always another excuse. Finally, I wised up. He didn't really love me. He loved having two mommies to take care of him.

The Trust-Fund Baby

Neil was forty-two and had never been married. He lived with his mother, and they even had a joint checking account. They were quite wealthy, so there was always plenty of money. Neil rarely held a steady job. He didn't have to work for the money, and he preferred to spend his time playing golf or tennis.

My life was very different. I was a working single mother with a ten-year-old daughter. I didn't have time to hang out at the club or

•

drop everything and run off on a whim. I guess Neil and I were completely unsuited for each other in that respect. But what really burned me was that he made no effort to understand my circumstances or help me out. His mother wasn't very nice to me either. She was one of those cool women who make you feel they expect you to curtsy and kiss their hand.

It was impossible from the start, but I was so attracted to Neil I hung on for eight months. By then he was starting to lose interest. He kept saying, "Lighten up—stop being so serious all the time." He wanted a party girl, and it wasn't me. I was a little bummed out at the time, but now I'm glad we broke up. My life is back to normal.

If worse comes to worst, you'll end up being his mother—making all the decisions, keeping home and hearth together, supporting him and comforting him when he's blue. Never mind if *you* feel down or have a bad day. This Mamma's Boy sucks all the energy out of you.

Kevin's Stunted Growth

I love Kevin to death, but he's not a self-starter. Although he has a degree in social

•

services, he's content to work part time as a security guard. He never does anything around the house. It's all left for me when I come home from a full day of work. Sometimes I think he wants a mother, not a lover.

It's as though he expects someone else to do everything for him—find him a job, take care of his needs and make him happy. This is not a mutual relationship at all. He needs to grow up and take charge of his own life. I know he has great potential, but I can push him only so far.

The irony is, I always thought I'd meet a man who would be an equal partner, and maybe even a little more aggressive than me. Instead, I have a child on my hands. Why don't I leave him? I can't answer that. My friends have all told me I should dump this wimp, but I see the spark of his greatness nobody else sees.

There's plenty of sorrow and misery for the wife or girlfriend of a Mama's Boy, but I had to laugh when I read the following letter. It was the perfect example—the ultimate jealous mother:

Carol, this is the nuttiest story you'll ever hear. Sonny's mother was so jealous of his

•

girlfriends that when he got engaged to me, she insisted on going with him to pick out my engagement ring. Then she forced his father to buy her the same ring but *with bigger diamonds*! Talk about being competitive!

•

Chapter Eight

·

The Batterer

*He Controls You with
a Fist*

*T*he voice on the Jerkline was almost a whisper.
"I need help," the woman said with desperation
in her voice. "Can you tell me what to do?"

I was a little nervous. I am not a psychotherapist
or a trained counselor, and I could immediately tell
she had a severe problem. I gently asked her what
was wrong.

"He hit me again," she whispered. "I hurt so much.
I'm sorry to bother you with this, but I saw you on

·

TV, and I thought maybe you could help me. Please—
I'm pregnant. I'm afraid for the baby."

I asked her if she was alone. It's dangerous for
battered women to make these kinds of calls if their
husbands or boyfriends are anywhere in the vicinity.
She told me her husband had gone to work.

"He hardly ever hits me anymore," she sniffed.
"Only when he gets really mad, or when he drinks. I
thought things were getting better."

I talked to her for a while, encouraging her to tell
her story. It was a typical case of a bullying husband
who used his fist to keep her in line. She told me she
tried to leave once, and when he found her, he beat
her within an inch of her life.

My heart went out to her. "I know you're feeling
very scared," I said. "And you may feel that you have
no choice but to stay with him and let him take care
of you, especially now that you're pregnant. But I
want you to know you have options. You don't have
to let him hit you. Get help. Do it for yourself, and
do it for your child."

I gave her the number of the National Battered
Women's Hotline (800-333-SAFE), and I pray that she
called and found help. I simply can't stand the idea
of women getting beaten by the men they love, but
it happens all the time.

The statistics are grim. Millions of women in this

•

country are being physically brutalized in their own homes. Listen to the evidence:

- One out of every four women will be battered in her lifetime.
- Physical violence occurs at least once in two thirds of all marriages.
- Domestic violence occurs among all races and socioeconomic groups.
- A woman is beaten every fifteen seconds in the United States.

One of the scariest things about Batterers is how often they appear outwardly to be normal, nice guys. No one would ever suspect that they are capable of abuse. I've heard from women who describe their husbands and boyfriends as pillars of the community, religious men, hard workers, highly educated professionals. It's a myth that only an ignorant, disreputable character would ever hit a woman.

The Batterer can also be the most charming guy you'd ever want to meet—a warm, loving friend, a reliable son and brother, everyone's favorite dinner guest. He's so good at wearing a mask of respectability and sanity that the woman he beats is frequently not believed when she finally tells the truth.

For those of you who shudder at the horrible idea

•

of being with such a man but then say, "It could never happen to me," think again. In the early stages of a relationship, the Batterer may appear to be your dream come true. It's very hard, if not impossible, to see the real person behind the mask. Hey, even Ted Bundy was a charmer!

But the "honeymoon" period of your relationship will end with a bang. Here's how a typical battering cycle begins:

1. He throws a temper tantrum. Maybe he hurls a plate against the wall or breaks another household item. Once he calms down, he'll seem embarrassed by the outburst and filled with remorse. He'll say, "I don't know what got into me. That case at work must really have frazzled my nerves. I'm so sorry, honey." Of course, you'll tell him to forget it. After all, everyone loses his temper once in a while.

2. The next time he loses his temper, he might break something that holds great sentimental value for you—a family heirloom or a personal memento. Since it has special meaning, it is irreplaceable. You are shocked and upset. It takes you a bit longer to forgive him.

•

Again, he melts you with the genuine nature of his remorse. He may even say, "I was angry and I wanted to hurt you, so I broke something you cared about. I'm so ashamed. How can you ever forgive me?" Of course you do forgive him. You're not one to carry a grudge, and you're still looking at this as an aberration of his normal behavior. You're probably willing to accept some of the blame, since your words or actions led to this scene in the first place.

3. For the first time, he will strike you— a slap or a punch. It may not be severe, and it certainly doesn't classify as a "battering." In fact, it may not even hurt you at all. You'll be upset, though, because he has stepped over a line of acceptability. The apologies that follow this attack will be especially profuse; he might even cry with shame, or promise to seek professional help. You forgive him, because you think it's an isolated incident, and he promises, "I will never lay a hand on you again."

Unless the Batterer does receive professional help— and even then the statistics are grim—and learns

•

what is at the basis of his need to control women with force, you'd better watch out. There is no such thing as a single incident. If he hit you once, he will hit you again. You can count on it. Over time the assaults will increase in frequency and severity, leaving you terrified of saying or doing anything that might set him off. Women who live with Batterers have told me these incidents follow a chillingly familiar course: First, they say, they can feel the tension mounting. As one woman described it, "There was a tightening in his jaw or mouth when he was annoyed. If I saw that happening, I immediately thought, Here it comes!" The self-protective instinct causes women to try to reduce the tension—to be especially compliant and gentle. But they can't control or predict what happens next. He is working his way up to a beating, and there is no way to stop him.

In the early days of physical abuse, the aftermath will bring long and impassioned apologies and pleas for forgiveness. As time goes on, however, even these will cease. You'll be locked in a vicious cycle.

Since Batterers are often such "normal" and even exceptional men, how can you spot one? There are some early warning signs. Read these questions and consider the man in your life:

• Does he have a noticeably bad temper?
  Does he often seem to overreact to the

•

slightest provocation? Has he ever thrown an item or broken something while he was angry? Does he behave in a Dr. Jekyll–Mr. Hyde manner—loving one moment, nasty the next?

- Was he raised in an abusive home? You shouldn't dismiss a man just because of his family history, but it is a factor that should be considered. Sons of abusers have a much greater chance of becoming abusers themselves, unless they have received counseling.

- Is he generally dismissive of women? Has he ever put you down in front of others with a comment such as, "Oh, it's just like a woman to say that?"

- Is he extremely jealous or possessive of you? Does he isolate you from family and friends, or insist on accompanying you when you go out? Initially, you may be flattered, but I assure you jealousy can turn to cruelty. In fact, it's one of the major warning signs of a potential physical abuser.

- Does he go out of his way to criticize others? Is he constantly voicing resentment toward people at work (especially his boss), family members or others? Does he say

•

things like, "I wish I could kick his ass" or describe the violence he would like to do to people?

• Does he abuse drugs or alcohol? Although alcohol and drug abuse are not the true causes of his behavior, they certainly can release his baser instincts. He will also have an excuse the next day: "I'm sorry, honey. I was drunk. I don't remember what happened." Don't believe it. He remembers.

• Has he ever threatened you with physical violence or spoken approvingly of men who "know how to put women in their place"?

• What types of friends does he have? Are all his buddies macho men who always have negative things to say about women?

If you are dating a man who exhibits any of these behaviors, I think you should run like hell. It isn't paranoid to say that you may end up in the hospital, a battered women's shelter or even in your grave if you don't take this threat seriously.

You may not be with a Batterer, but maybe you have a friend who is. Now that you're aware of the patterns, I urge you to keep them in mind if any

•

woman you're close to begins to act in a way that suggests abuse. Maybe you can reach out to her.

The signs are there for those who understand the syndrome, but most of us don't see them. Now that you know, consider: Has your formerly outgoing friend stopped calling you? Does she seem nervous or reluctant to engage in more than cursory conversation? If you get together, does he insist on accompanying her? Does she wear unusually heavy makeup or dresses with long sleeves even in the middle of summer? Is she bruised or hurt in any way? If so, are her excuses vague and not very plausible ("I fell down." "I ran into a table.")?

Your friend may be physically abused, but you can't just ask her straight out and expect her to admit it. It is impossible to comprehend the degree of terror and shame a battered woman feels, not to mention how important it may be for her that everyone see her relationship in a favorable light.

If you want to help her, be gentle and persistent. Sometimes it's enough to let someone know she has a friend—a person to call if things get out of control.

The women who wrote or called about physically abusive men had horrifying stories to tell. Nearly all of them had one thing in common: They had no idea, until they were deep into the relationship, that the man of their dreams was really the man of their night-

•

mares. Their stories will shock you, and if you're like me, they will move you to tears.

The Brutal Hunter

I married my second husband in December of 1978 when I was fifty-six years old. I was seven years older than Ray, but that didn't bother him. We both had good jobs, and we had a lot in common. Ray was a great golfer, and he shared my love of fishing and camping.

There was no sign of a temper, mean streak or excessive drinking during our first year to-gether. Over time, I began to notice Ray was hitting the sauce a little too much. When I mentioned it, he threw a dinner plate at the wall, barely missing my head. I was stunned. That wasn't my Ray.

The first time he hit me, it was to slap me very hard in the face—so hard my jaw tingled for hours. I fled from the room and closed myself in the bedroom, crying my heart out. Later he came in, sober and remorseful. We talked for a long time. He told me how frus-trated he was at work and apologized profusely for taking it out on me. I felt so bad for him. I didn't want him to suffer. I forgave him, and we made beautiful love that night.

•

Sadly, it didn't end there, as I had hoped and expected. During the next two years, there were many loud, screaming battles where he would throw things against the wall and hit or kick me. The apartment manager finally came to say the neighbors were complaining, and he would have to throw us out if it kept up. I was so humiliated to think others were hearing all of this, but Ray wasn't the least bit embarrassed. He demanded to know who had complained, so he could take care of it himself. I could see his rage was completely out of bounds, but what could I do? Leave him? I was almost sixty years old. I truly believed I would stay with him until he killed me.

Everything changed when my daughter came for a visit. She had not seen me since Ray and I were married, and on the second day of her visit she pulled me aside and said with alarm, "Mother, I can tell something horrible is wrong. What is it?" I couldn't help myself. I burst into tears and told her the whole story. She was a bundle of cold fury as she listened. "I'd like to kill that man," she said, "but I'm more interested in you. We've got to get you out of here." She called her husband, who is a real sweetie, and told him

•

the situation. They insisted I pack my bags and come stay with them. I hesitated, but my daughter would not take no for an answer. She said, "Either you come with me or I'm calling the police."

We planned my "escape" while Ray was at work the next day. I wrote him a long letter explaining my reasons for leaving.

That was two years ago. I won't go into all the messiness of what transpired after I left. Suffice it to say that the unpleasantness of divorcing Ray couldn't hold a candle to the horror of living with him. I thank God every day for my daughter, who made me leave. Sometimes I ask myself whether I'd handle things the same way if I had to do it all over again. I can't honestly answer. You get so sucked into a way of life until even the most outrageous things seem perfectly normal. All I can say now is that no woman deserves to be hit by a man. I hope your readers who are in abusive relationships will not wait as long as I did to get out.

Life with a Monster

My relationship was a ten-year nightmare. I left him two years ago, and I still feel shaky.

•

It's like I'm recovering from an awful disease. Here are some of the things he did:

He threw food or drink at me many times.

He tore up my clothes if he thought they weren't in good taste, and constantly harangued me about how I was dressed.

He broke my nose.

He slapped me around every time I stepped out of line the least bit.

I could go on, but I think you get the picture. Believe it or not, I loved him, but in the end I stayed with him out of fear.

When I finally left, I gave no forwarding address. It was only the love and support of a new man, who is now my fiancé, that helped me through the pain. I see now that I was weak, but I've changed. I will never again allow a man to hit me, use me, or emotionally abuse me. Not for as long as I live!

We know that physical abuse is about as far as you can get from love. But in the beginning, obsessive control can seem like the most complete form of flattery. The jealous husband in the next story could not control his escalating rage:

•

Carol Rosen

Jealousy Gone Berserk

I met John through friends, and I fell madly, passionately, desperately in love with him. I never had a clue there was anything strange about him. To the contrary, he treated me like I was made of solid gold. He was also funny and very bright, and our conversations were almost as exciting to me as our wonderful sex. When he proposed, I couldn't believe how lucky I was to land such a wonderful man. Naturally, I said yes.

After our marriage, John became very possessive, but in a sweet way. He told me he couldn't stand the thought of losing me or of anything happening to me. I felt so protected and loved. Still, it seemed he carried things a bit far; he was paranoid about my walking to the corner grocery, for fear someone would jump out of a bush. At first I laughed and reminded him that I was all grown up and able to take care of myself. Eventually, however, it became less amusing. I was annoyed by his possessiveness and wanted to tell him, "Get a life! Stop following my every move."

It all came to a head one evening when I stopped at a bar on the way home from work

•

to have a drink with a friend. John hadn't worked that day, so I'd called him at home and left a message on our answering machine that I would be late. I had one glass of wine and spent no more than an hour at the bar. However, when I walked in the door, you'd think I was stumbling in drunk at three A.M. He lunged at me and grabbed me by the hair, pinning me against the wall. He was screaming, "Who were you with, bitch, who were you with?" over and over. Then he grabbed me and choked me until I passed out. When I awoke, I was in shock. I couldn't believe this had happened to me.

I went to work the next day, and my supervisor noticed my bruises. I'll never forget her kindness. She told me, "If you don't leave him, we'll be reading about your murder in the papers." She gave me time off to go look for an apartment. I found one, and on a night when he wasn't home, I packed my things and left with no forwarding address. I was lucky because he never tried to find me, and besides a quick appearance at our divorce hearing, I never heard from him again. Some of the women I met in a battered women's support group I joined weren't so lucky.

•

Even if you're strong enough to cry foul, you still have to contend with the disbelief of others. Remember, the Batterer might be seen by them as a perfect saint; he saves his vicious hobbies for private. He also might be well connected. The woman who wrote me this letter felt defeated for years by the fact that her husband and his family were so socially prominent she was sure no one would believe her.

The Ultimate Power Struggle

My husband slapped and hit me regularly, and one time he shoved the butt of a deer rifle in my face. Even during sex—I wouldn't call it "making love"—he bruised me internally with his roughness. But I was helpless because his family was prominent and politically powerful in our community. I knew nobody would believe me.

It got scarier and scarier—like living in a sick, twisted horror movie. One night I got so scared I locked him out of the house. He slit the screen door with a hunting knife, then he bounded into the room and pushed the tip of the knife into my stomach. I froze, knowing if I moved he'd kill me.

I finally broke down at a family gathering, and I think it saved my life. Everyone was

•

talking and laughing, and I just blurted out, "Your son beats me, and I'm afraid he's going to kill me. What's wrong with you people— can't you see it?" There wasn't a sound in the room, then things happened very fast. His parents whisked me into a private room and demanded I tell them everything. By the end of the evening, it was decided my husband would be sent away for treatment. His father asked me if I wanted a divorce. I said yes, and he said, "Don't worry, we'll take care of it. There's no need for any of this to be discussed outside this room." I felt like I was accepting a bribe for my silence, but I didn't care. As long as I got out alive, that's all that mattered.

I think the saddest truth about physically abused women is how hard it is for them to get protection against the men who hurt them. I don't want you to be discouraged if you need to get away from a Batterer, but you may as well know: It's a tough process— especially if you have children. This woman's story really tore me up. It's almost beyond belief.

Nobody Cares

Brenda called the Jerkline and said, "Did you know it's legal to lie in court?"

•

women. They think we're all hysterical, over-reacting bitches. Meanwhile, we're being beaten, our children are being abused and no-body cares. After what we went through, I've become totally cynical about our so-called system of justice. Try explaining justice to my little boy!

If you are with a Batterer, it will be hard to get free. But no matter how hard it is, I believe you will find it's worth the effort. By taking legal action or leaving, you may be saving your life. And, God knows, you'll be saving your sanity.

It's important to have the facts before you take action. Here are some general points to keep in mind as you plan your escape:

Just because you've called a shelter doesn't mean you have to leave. Many shelters offer programs for Batterers and their spouses or girlfriends. The goal of these programs is to help the Batterer understand the trauma he is causing and to change his behavior.

A shelter will also give you advice about your options, such as having a protective or restraining order placed against the man who is beating you. The people at the shelter will also know how well such orders are enforced in your community. This may make it possible for you to remain in your home. Such an order forbids him to come near you under the threat of

•

arrest. It won't always stop a Batterer, but sometimes it's a workable solution.

If you've called your shelter and have decided to leave, or have arranged for an order of protection, take no action against your abuser. It may place you in extreme danger if he learns you are planning to leave. Don't tell anyone else who might deliberately or inadvertently tell him. Sometimes, even good friends or family members, acting with the best of intentions, will try to "patch things up." They may not realize how dangerous the situation has become for you. What you are experiencing is not a normal "lover's quarrel." It's severe abuse.

Always remember, you're not alone. Statistics show that between three million and four million women are battered every year by their husbands or partners. Once you see that your situation is shared by others, you can let go of the feeling that somehow you have caused this to happen and that you are a bad person. This is the first step to recovery.

No matter what your Batterer says, you are not to blame. He is the one with the problem, not you. He would treat any woman in the same way—and probably has a history of doing just that. Remember that a physical abuser is often an expert at psychological abuse. He may tell you, "If you did your job and were a better wife, I wouldn't get so furious." Or, "How can you expect me to control myself when you do

•

things that drive me crazy?" *It is not your fault that he beats you.*

The question keeps coming up, over and over again, "Why do these women stay?" It's simply beyond the understanding of anyone who hasn't lived through the situation. Maybe you stay for one of these reasons:

- He can follow you anywhere—and often threatens to do so. You don't feel any safer leaving than you do staying. You might have left once, and he followed you to where you were staying and made an ugly scene. Later, after you got home, he gave you a beating that made his former abuse seem like child's play.
- He tells you he'll take your children away from you if you go. He'll threaten to have you declared an unfit mother.
- Over time your friends have become alienated, so you don't feel close enough to them to ask for help. If they're his friends, too, you're afraid they won't believe you since he puts on such a mask of sanity in front of everyone else but you.
- The police won't help unless you press charges. Even if you do, they can't guarantee he'll stay away or never hurt you again.

•

• You feel overwhelmed, terrified and hopeless.

Whatever the reason, neither fear nor shame needs to control you. It is your right, given to you at birth, to live in safety. If you are with a Batterer now, I implore you to call the National Battered Women's Hotline (800-333-SAFE) or your local police station to find a shelter in your area. Shelters have helped thousands of women, and they'll help you as you begin your journey to safety and freedom.

•

Chapter Nine

The Addict

He Makes Life a Nightmare

*W*ayne was an all-purpose jerk. He was insanely jealous, beat his wife, Jean, on many occasions and was overly dependent on his mother. But there was one factor that dominated the rest: Wayne was an alcoholic. All his other behavior could be traced to his drinking.

That was the conclusion I reached when I talked to Jean on the Jerkline. She told me a long tale of abuse and despair. "You've heard it before, I'm sure," she said wearily. "He started out being a great guy

·

and turned into a monster after we got married. Wayne could go through a fifth of vodka and half a case of beer a night without passing out. Actually, it was a relief if he did pass out. It was certainly better than having him awake and mean.

"Every night it was the same story. He'd drink, I'd wait for whatever new humiliation was coming. He had a little game he'd play. He'd ask for my opinion about something, using this sugary-sweet voice. When I answered, he'd rage at me, belittle me and tell me how stupid I was. Still, that wasn't as bad as the beatings, which took place for any reason or no reason. He hit me if I put the toilet paper in the wrong way.

"Wayne's mother blamed me for everything. She said he was a decent man before he met me. Once she said, 'What have you done to my son?' By that point, I was pretty much at my wit's end. I shot back, 'Your darling son urinated all over the wall this morning. Didn't you ever toilet-train him?' "

I asked her, "Did you leave him?"

She sighed. "Yeah, finally. Our divorce just came through last month, but I'm not completely rid of him. He'll still call me at three in the morning to go on a drunken tirade. I'm going to get an unlisted number."

I was curious about how she was doing emotionally. "What did this experience do to you?"

•

She answered seriously. "I know alcoholism is a disease. I also know it's not my fault Wayne drinks, but I've seen a side of life I never knew existed. Before Wayne, I hadn't known one alcoholic in my life. I had no idea how complicated this disease could be. I do know one thing, though. It may sound cold, but this isn't my problem. Finding that out was my big breakthrough."

As Jean discovered, being with an Addict is its own special hell. There's no other experience like it.

As with other types of jerks, however, you can't always spot an Addict at the beginning of a relationship. Here's why:

- He's in a state of denial about his problem. He might realize he drinks a lot or uses drugs more than just casually, but he doesn't believe it's an uncontrollable problem. He boasts, "I can quit anytime." He might accuse you of being a stick-in-the-mud, saying, "Everyone needs to let off steam sometimes."
- He is supported by a society that condones and even encourages the use of alcohol and, depending on what circles you travel in, some recreational drugs. People who

•

don't drink are considered strange or called party poopers.
- He may be surrounded by other Addicts, and they all support each other's behavior. They'll shun anyone who disapproves.
- If he's like most Addicts, he's very good at hiding his habit. This is especially easy if you're not familiar with the physical and emotional signs of substance abuse.

Fortunately, substance abuse is no longer the dirty little secret it once was. Today, there are many places to get help, and I'm not just talking about help for the Addict. I'm talking about help for you, the woman whose life has been ravaged by his disease. In recent years, alcohol and drug counselors have discovered that addictions are family diseases, and each person in the Addict's family develops his or her own "disease" as a reaction to his problem. You may become a "codependent" or an enabler. This means your life becomes unmanageable because of his habit. You berate and nag to no avail. You constantly make excuses for him to friends and family. You call in sick for him when he has a hangover. In the worst case, you may lift him out of a pool of his own vomit and drag him to bed.

You do all of these things out of love, but none of

•

them helps him get well. Each time you cover up, clean up or fix a situation caused by his addiction, you enable him to keep drinking or doing drugs. He never has to face the consequences of his addiction, because you're there to face them for him. If there's one message for enablers, it's this: You don't have to pity a man and become his girlfriend, lover or wife simply because he can't take care of himself. He may be heartbroken, sick, lonely and depressed, but you can't cure him. That's his decision. The person you have to take care of is *yourself*!

If you have children, they get sucked in by the disease as well. Children are very sensitive, and they see and hear more than you think. If their dad is drinking and being abusive, they may blame themselves and think all this craziness is caused by something they've done wrong. What happens is that your whole family—you and the children—are living every moment in the shadow of his addiction. You never take care of your own needs, and your children get shortchanged in receiving the love and attention they deserve.

Imagine their worries: "What if Dad comes to the school play drunk?" "Can I have a friend over to the house to play or will *he* be there?" "Is he going to hit me?" The list goes on and on. You may not be aware of their fears because they keep them inside. They're probably worried about you, too. They can

•

see you're hurting, and they don't want to hurt you any further. But be aware of the consequences if you and your children don't get help. Current statistics show that 50 percent of children with one addictive parent and 80 percent of children with two addictive parents are likely to become Addicts themselves. Even if they escape that fate, they're more likely than other people to get into relationships with alcoholics and drug abusers.

You can break the cycle, and you're lucky to have so many organizations that offer help. (Most of them are listed in Appendix A.) Don't hesitate a minute longer: Call and make a start. Know that your situation is not hopeless. Know that even if you can't change your partner's behavior, you can change your own life.

Most of the women who contacted me about their Addict partners did find a way out, even though sometimes it followed years of suffering. Their stories are painful, but they can also be an inspiration. Tess, the woman in the following story, spent many years coming to terms with her husband's terrible addiction:

Reign of Terror

"I was raised in Mississippi in a healthy, old-fashioned family," Tess told me on the Jerkline. "I knew nothing about drugs. I just knew about normal things, like

•

work, school, church and family. I grew up in a rural area, but Ron had been in the army and had seen more of life." Tess continued:

> I was young and naïve, but I knew I loved this man, and he was crazy about me. We were married after he got out of the army. He started a good-paying government job in Chicago, and I got pregnant. We named our baby daughter Angie.
>
> Things went along fine for a few years, until Ron became frustrated with his job. He knew he'd never advance without a degree, so I went to work so he could go to college. I just about worshiped him, and I would have given my life to see him succeed.
>
> I don't remember exactly when things started going downhill. I was working, and Angie was in day care. Ron was at school, but often when I got home from work, he'd be sitting with friends in our apartment, and I had the impression they'd been partying. He also went out sometimes at night, saying he had to let off steam. He told me he was down at the pool hall.
>
> So many things seemed out of whack, but I couldn't put my finger on what was wrong. Then I found out.

•

One day when I went to get the mail, I found several foil packets in the mailbox. Somehow I knew it was a kind of drug, even though I had no idea what. Anyway, I hid the packets. When Ron came home, he seemed very upset. He asked me if I had checked the mailbox. I told him no. He went crazy that night, and I knew it was because of the missing drugs. It scared me.

Next I found a hypodermic needle in his underwear drawer. By now I had done some reading, and I was really worried. But the worst thing was finding the burned spoon. I had read that heroin addicts used spoons. My husband was a heroin addict! My God, I was worried.

The next day, I called a drug hotline and spoke to a counselor. He confirmed that all the signs were there. I'm ashamed to say I did nothing. I couldn't think of a way to approach Ron about this. I was too scared. But things kept getting crazier. He would cash my paycheck, then tell me he'd been robbed on his way home from the bank. He started staying out all night. I suspected he wasn't going to classes. Things got so bad I called my mother and asked her if Angie and I could come and

•

stay with her. I told Ron I was leaving, and he didn't even seem to hear me.

We went down to Georgia, and I got a job there. Ron didn't call me for about five months. Then he called and begged me to come back. He admitted he had been using drugs, but promised me he'd stopped. I believed him and was thrilled, but that was only the beginning. Over the next six years, Ron was in and out of rehab four times, and each time he ended up back on heroin. That stuff is so powerful—I can't even imagine it. The last year we were together, everything deteriorated. He had lost all sense of reality and all control. He'd stumble home and urinate on the floor.

That's when I left him for good. I did it for Angie, and also for myself. I broke off all contact with him, and today I don't know whether he's alive or dead. When I think of how promising our life once was, I just want to cry.

Today, Angie is doing fine. This child is the light of my life. I'll tell you one thing. I never bad-mouthed her daddy to her. A child has to have some respect for her parents, even if they're bums. I always told Angie Daddy was

•

sick, and he couldn't help himself because of his disease. It's the truth. I don't want Angie to hate her father. I don't hate him. I feel sorry for him. It's all a big waste of life.

Tess didn't know Ron was a user when she married him, but what about women who *do* know and get involved with Addicts anyway? Why do they do it? There are many reasons, but one might be that these men seem, at first sight, to be more exciting and adventurous than other men. They can be big party animals, make you laugh and take you on a whirlwind ride. The woman who wrote the next letter was attracted to her Addict because he wasn't boring; he lifted her from the ordinary. But she was in for an awful crash.

The Bad-News Bouncer

I met Lance in a bar where he worked as a bouncer. I noticed right away he had a fierce temper, but somehow it was part of his intrigue. I'd never been with such a physical man before. It was exciting.

I didn't even suspect he did drugs until after we were married, although I knew he drank a lot. But the drugs did him in. He'd get "sick"—his way of saying he needed a fix. He

•

was always trying to con doctors into giving him medication for imaginary back pain or whatever else he could think of.

Finally, I was exhausted from the effort, and I saw I had made a very big mistake. I got out before he had done too much damage. God knows what will become of him, but I'm not about to be his nursemaid.

The Addict rarely has just one problem. If there's such a thing as an "addictive personality," he has it. He might be drinking heavily, using drugs, gambling and even be a sexaholic. The woman who wrote me this letter got the shock of her life when she learned her boyfriend was bigger trouble than she'd imagined:

Three-for-One

I was in a so-called committed relationship with this man for almost three years. He was a recovering alcoholic and drug abuser. During the three years, we broke up about three times. He'd get to a certain point, then get scared and back up. I found that very hard to deal with. After all, I loved him very much and wanted to spend the rest of my life with him. I believed eventually we'd get married.

Then he had a relapse, and that was pretty

•

unpleasant. But I helped him through it. I was the biggest codependent on two feet! As I think back on it now, I'm disgusted. He was an ace at manipulation and intimidation. I think he wrote the book on both. He had me at his beck and call. Then something horrible happened to end the relationship.

Carol, you're not going to believe this one. He turned out to be three addictive personalities rolled into one. Let me explain. I had gone to the doctor for my regular pap smear, and she found an abnormality, which she told me was a sexually transmitted disease. Well, there's only one way that could have happened! I confronted my boyfriend, but he denied everything. I felt I could no longer trust him, so I broke up with him. Then I found out from some of my friends at the Alcoholics Anonymous group he attended that he was seducing and then dumping new members on a regular basis. Some of those women never came back to AA. "Your boyfriend is a sex addict," one woman told me. "He's transferred his addiction to alcohol and drugs to an addiction to sex—that's his new high."

Carol, I can't tell you how hurt and upset I was. There I was, sitting at home thinking he was at meetings to help himself, when all

•

he was doing was cheating on me! He's tried to get back together with me, but I'm *definitely* not interested.

One woman who called the Jerkline was disgusted with herself. "My dad was an alcoholic," she said. "I can't believe I married one! I must be the dumbest woman alive." I assured her that wasn't true. If anything, she was the norm. As I've said before, children of Addicts have a far greater chance of getting involved with or marrying Addicts when they reach adulthood. One reason is because they have grown up being enablers, and they are drawn to men who need rescuing. In this way, they continue the pattern of enabling that has become their primary identity. Sometimes they just fall into it. I found the following woman's story particularly heartbreaking. She was so abused as a child that she escaped blindly right into the arms of another Addict.

The Vicious Cycle

My father was an alcoholic. My mother had to marry him because she got pregnant with me—a fact she never let me forget. She enjoyed telling me how she tried to abort me. Nice, huh? Between the two of them, my parents made my life a nightmare of fear. They

•

were both physically and emotionally abusive. I wasn't allowed to have friends over, go places or date boys. Our house was my prison.

My mother treated me like a slave and made me responsible for taking care of my younger brothers. I had never even been on a date when I met Louis. He started calling me, and I managed to sneak around with him behind my parents' backs. I was desperate to get away from them, even though I was only seventeen and hadn't finished high school. And Louis was no prize. He could go through a six-pack of beer in record time. Still, being with him was better than living at home.

But when I married Louis, I jumped from the frying pan into the fire. He couldn't keep a job, he beat me up and he verbally abused me. I had no money and no place to run to. I certainly couldn't go back to my parents. I was only eighteen, and I felt like an old woman. I even contemplated suicide. What point was there in going on?

Then a friend told me about Al-Anon. I snuck off to a meeting, and it changed my life. Suddenly, I was hearing things about what people who drink can do to you. I was hearing it wasn't my fault. A woman in the group hooked me up with another organiza-

•

tion for children of alcoholics. I began to understand what had happened to me while I was growing up.

Nobody in the groups ever told me I should divorce Louis. They left it up to me to decide what to do. It took time, but I finally realized he wasn't going to change and that I deserved a better life. It was time to stop repeating the past, so I divorced him and am living on my own now. And you know what? I think I'm going to make it.

Good for her! You can see how much bravery these women exhibit. I admire them so much. It makes me feel especially good when I hear about women who got out and made a statement to the world. They stood up and shouted, "I count!" Here's a very inspiring example:

A woman left this message on the Jerkline: "I hear you're looking for jerks. My ex-husband was a superjerk. Would you like to know how I got his name in the headlines?"

Intrigued, I called her back. Rosalie, a forty-six-year-old woman who was married for many years to a drug addict, told me how she and her children were forced to beg for food, live in homeless shelters and suffer countless indignities after they fled from the crazed Addict. She said:

•

I was so angry. We were just another statistic, as far as people were concerned. All I wanted was a little help, but the services were pathetic. I got so mad, I started writing letters. I wrote to the president, congressmen, senators—all the people who are supposed to be representing our interests. I read them the riot act. I told them, "Look at us. We are the victims of drug abuse. We are not the users; we are the victims."

Finally, a local newspaper columnist called me and offered to write a feature telling my story. I was glad to oblige. And I used my real name, plus my ex-husband's real name. I wanted to send a message that men can't get away with this. It's time for people to take responsibility for their actions—and for all of us to take care of each other.

•

people have asked, "Why do women allow
lves to get into this predicament in the first
In my research, I've discovered six main rea-
hy women get involved with jerks and why they
en when things are bad for years.

ou're wondering, "How did I get into this
" you might consider one of the following fac-

You Don't Believe in Yourself

are now learning more and more about why
have problems with self-esteem. Often the
can be traced to their upbringing in dysfunc-
families. A dysfunctional family is one in which
does not receive the love and nurture he or
eeds. By the time you reach adulthood, you are
g around with what experts call "a hole in your
Deep down, you feel that something is missing.
ause of this emptiness, you will seek the things
idn't get as a child. But all along, you're stuck
the notion that you are a bad or defective per-
-that somehow you are responsible for all the
s that happened to you. It is not unusual for
en of alcoholics or drug abusers to blame them-
s, thinking, If I am a better kid, Mommy won't
to drink. This is a classic example of blaming
ictim instead of the offender.

•

Chapter Ten

•

Getting Free

*There's Always
a Way Out*

*M*arlene was married for thirty years to a man
who abused her physically and emotionally. She
described to me when she called the Jerkline how she
had tolerated endless criticism, escalating to bruises
and even a bloody nose. "He laughed when our daughter asked what happened to me and told her, 'She ran
into my hand.' It was a big joke to him. He was
completely smug about his ability to control me. And
for a long time, I bowed to his every wish, desperately

•

trying to keep the peace. But in my heart, I knew someday I would find a way to leave."

For years, Marlene squirreled away money from her household account, planning her escape. It didn't come until the children were grown, but by then she was determined to leave. "Carol," she said, "I was fifty-six years old, and I knew it was my last chance. I had a choice: I could stay with him and go to my grave abused and unhappy. Or I could try to grab a little happiness for myself. I had no desire to meet a new man and get married again. I just wanted to be free. I fantasized about what it would be like to get up in the morning and not have to face his criticism. Or to fix dinner without fearing I would get hit if it wasn't perfect. My dreams of a new life kept me going through the worst times."

Finally, she was ready to make her move. Marlene described to me how she secretly rented an apartment with the money she had saved and got a secretarial job that earned her enough to pay expenses.

I hadn't worked for thirty years, but I had been brushing up on my typing skills in preparation for leaving.

When I had everything set, I told him I was leaving. I chose a busy restaurant, because I was so afraid of his rage. He created quite a scene anyway, calling me every name in the

•

book. He seemed to t
I would be nothing
all I had been throu
most painful of my l

When I left, I had
was hard, but such a
from me. Now I'm ju
get all the terrible tl
me. Every day, they f
into the past. Sure, it
and society makes yo
without a man. But
happy, and I'm beginn
than I ever thought I
help. I think He wan
their full potential. Y
you're being abused.

I was moved by Marlene's
Here was a woman who hac
her. She might easily have
horrible man forever, but sl
on my mind long after I hu
thinking, If she can do it, a

For most of this book,
experiences of women who
ships with jerks. Now I wa
important message of all: Yc

Man
thems
place?
sons w
stay, e

If y
mess?
tors:

We
people
roots
tional
a chil
she n
walki
soul.'

Be
you
with
son—
thing
child
selve
have
the

•

In the worst cases of physical or sexual abuse, you may have felt you were terrible and dirty. And perhaps your parents reinforced this idea by constantly telling you that you were stupid, ugly and not worthy of love.

Your mind works like a computer, and the negative messages get stored as data. You internalize the cruel barbs and carry them with you into adulthood.

How does this lead you into relationships with jerks? You might think it's normal to be put down and abused. As hard as it is to believe, what is familiar is sometimes more comfortable than what is unfamiliar. Maybe you're afraid of true, honest love. You think you deserve to lead a miserable life.

Maybe you're afraid of getting close to another person because you think, If he finds out what I'm really like, he'll leave me. Years of hearing that you're worthless have worn away your ability to see yourself clearly or to recognize your goodness.

You Can't Face the Repetition of Past Hurts

Sometimes people carry the anger and pain from a previous relationship into a new relationship. If you've had several relationships with jerks, you may have reached the conclusion that all men are like this. We tend to experience what we expect and reject what doesn't fit into our expectations.

•

Carol Rosen

Some of the women who have contacted me sound like broken dolls—hurt and vulnerable, with no hope of recovery. They say that they will never trust another man. They are scared to death of risking a new relationship because they don't believe they'll ever find happiness. This is so sad. Bad men have damaged them so much they can't open themselves to the good things that can be theirs when they finally heal.

You Are Deeply Afraid of Being Alone

Everything in our society is built around couples. If you don't have a man in your life, you are made to feel less than whole. The message is constantly reinforced that we can only feel good in the presence of another person—preferably a handsome, romantic man. Have you ever seen a toothpaste commercial with the script, "My breath feels fresh. Great! Now I'll go take a walk on the beach by myself"? No. The person is always joined by a romantic partner, and they kiss and stroll off into the sunset together. These are the images we have been raised on. We're supposed to feel incomplete if we don't have a partner.

Women are judged as successes or failures based on their relationships. Even if they succeed in other ways, the question "Why isn't she married?" is always hanging in the air. When I started the Jerkline and appeared on TV, I was very excited about what I was

•

accomplishing, and I expected my family to be excited, too. But after viewing a tape of my television appearances, my grandfather said, "Nice—but when are you going to get married?" No one seems to care whether you're in a good or bad relationship—only if you are married. Well, that's wrong.

As you move into your twenties and thirties, the pressure increases. The refrain is repeated at parties and family gatherings: "When are you going to settle down with a nice man?" All around you, friends are getting married and having children. That's the "normal" thing to do. So what's wrong with you?

In a corner of our minds, each of us fears being alone. But does that mean we have to settle for a jerk? The strongest message I have heard from women who left bad relationships was this: "I am happier alone than I was with him."

The underlying issue is self-esteem. If you can say, "I'm fine just the way I am," or "I can live a satisfying life without a man, " then you are ready to find a *real* relationship—one in which there is mutual love and support.

You Are Financially and Emotionally Dependent

Staying with a jerk may seem your only recourse if you don't have the money or skills to make it on

•

your own. Maybe you have small children, or are an older woman who has never worked outside the home. What can you do? I sympathize with women who have described circumstances that would daunt any normal person. None of us can truly appreciate the hardships some people face. All I can say is, even when things seem impossible, if you are determined to be independent, there is a way. There are people you can talk to and phone numbers you can call (some of which appear in Appendix A of this book). You may believe you're alone, but I urge you not to become discouraged.

You Were Conned by the Jerk "Bait and Switch" Technique

Many jerks, particularly the hard-line types such as Batterers, Critics, Con Men, etc., are masters of deception and bad behavior. One question I always ask the women who call the Jerkline is, "Were there any signs when you were in the initial stages of your relationship that things would turn out the way they did?"

In an overwhelming majority of cases, the answer was no. In the few cases where there were some warning signs, they were so insignificant (For example, one woman said, "Well, he kicked the dog once.") that the women dismissed them.

•

These men may seem like the best thing that ever happened to you in the beginning. I've heard hundreds of tales of wildly romantic courtships, men who were loving and sensitive—the perfect mate— until the women married or moved in with them. Then the jerks showed their true colors. Naturally, by then the women were emotionally and/or financially dependent on them and it was very difficult for them to get out of the relationship.

I still remember a chilling conversation I had with David Garvin, who is the director of Alternatives to Domestic Aggression, a Batterer's counseling program of Catholic Social Services of Washtenaw County, Michigan. I said to David, "What really gets me about these guys is how they can be so nice at first. But once they've got the women, they turn into monsters!" I'll never forget Dave's reply. "You don't understand, Carol. They're *never* nice guys. They use a part of their personalities to trap the women so that they can begin to batter them."

To avoid this trap, pay close attention to the behavior and background of any man you're getting serious about. Love does *not* have to be blind. Nobody is perfect, but certain behaviors are the warning signs of disaster to follow. I hope that reading this book has given you some good information on the warning signs of men who go beyond "just being human." Always remember that *actions* speak louder than

•

words. I also advise you to "go with your gut." If you have a feeling that something is wrong, there probably is. Check it out before you allow the relationship to go any further.

You Are Influenced
by Religious Convictions

It's hard to justify your desire to leave a marriage if your religion decrees that you are together "for better or for worse, until death." I can't give you much advice except to say it is my opinion that God wants each of us to fulfill our full potential as individuals. I have no argument with any religion. I only believe everyone has a right to know love, peace and happiness.

Whatever your reasons are for being with a jerk, there is always a way out. I know there is because I found a way to leave *my* jerk, and I have spoken to countless women who did the same. All of us are much happier today than we would have been had we stayed.

The following stories are precious because they are from women who somehow found enough strength and the inner resources to get free. I hope they are an inspiration to you.

•

Linda's Recovery

I was married to an alcoholic for twenty-six years. For a long time, I didn't think I had any choices, because in the 1950s there wasn't much help available for women. You just stayed in the marriage and learned to live with it.

I finally got a divorce in 1978, and it was the most wonderful feeling I had experienced in my life. It was as if someone opened a window and let the fresh air wash over me.

But as glad as I am to be free, I am still haunted by the thought of how living the way we did affected my children. They have grown into good people, but I know they have been emotionally hurt. My son doesn't really trust anyone, and my daughter has been in a series of bad relationships. All those years, I stayed with a jerk for the sake of my children. Now I realize it was a mistake. If I had to do it all over again, I would have left this man the first time he got drunk and said a cruel word to me. I hope other women are smarter than I was.

One woman's self-esteem was so low she thought her angry, critical husband was the only man who

•

would want her. A friend at work made her feel desirable again and helped her find the self-assurance she needed to leave the brute:

Marie's Turning Point

I met my husband in high school, and our relationship was volatile from the start. Dennis had a terrible temper and threw tantrums if he didn't get his own way. I broke off the engagement twice but finally married him because he promised to change—and I really did love him.

For the first year, we fought constantly. I realized something was wrong. Normal people didn't live like this. I was walking on eggs all the time. I never knew what would set him off. I felt worthless and unhappy.

Then a man I worked with began to show an interest in me. Sometimes we'd have lunch together, and we laughed and talked about everything. I wouldn't have dreamed of getting involved with him on anything but a "just friends" basis, but our friendship changed me. I felt more attractive, desirable and interesting than I had ever felt with Dennis. It was this

•

relationship that gave me the courage to leave
my marriage after six years.

The hardest thing I had to do was tell my
mother I was getting a divorce. She's a devout
Catholic, and I was afraid she would react
badly. To my astonishment, she responded,
"What took you so long?"

The best news is that three years after my
divorce, I met a wonderful man who has made
life a joy. I'm now pregnant with our second
child, and I couldn't be happier. I shudder to
think that I might have stayed with Dennis
and never experienced the joy my husband
and child give me every day.

One woman had to come to terms with her relationship with a controlling, abusive father before she
could confront her equally controlling husband:

Taking On Two Men

It took me many frustrating years of therapy
to understand what my father did to me. I
endured years of suffering at his hands, and
what hurt the most about his criticism and
disapproval was that I idolized him. He put
me down constantly, and nothing I did was

•

ever right. I spent my life trying to please him.

Wouldn't you know, I married a man just like my father, and the pattern continued. My salvation was an understanding therapist who helped me to consider my own needs and feelings, for the first time in my life. She encouraged me to look at myself in a new way and see that I didn't deserve all the criticism and disrespect. Now I can stand up to my father—and my husband, too. I've put them both on notice that I will no longer listen to their constant harping. What's interesting is that both of them insist they never meant to hurt me. They were just trying to help me be a better person. Some men are so twisted! My response to this baloney was to tell them both, in my most sarcastic voice, "Don't do me any favors."

Not every woman wants or needs professional therapy, but sometimes it can be a woman's salvation, cutting through years of self-disgust and fear. Here's the story of another woman who was brought back to life after her marriage broke up:

•

A New Lease on Life

My husband left me after twenty-two years of marriage. I didn't realize how bad things had been until he was gone. I now see that his leaving was the best thing that could have happened to me. I was very dependent on him. During our marriage, I was always doing what I was told, and trying to be the perfect wife.

I was very lucky because I had a group of friends who supported me. They dragged me kicking and screaming into the twentieth century. They convinced me to see a therapist, and that was the best thing I ever did for myself. She helped me express my anger about all the ways my husband had controlled and abused me over the years. Today I am truly myself for the first time in my life. I can look in the mirror and see a terrific, lively, attractive woman. I can't tell you what a great victory this is!

If you believe that all men are jerks and you'll never be lucky enough to find a decent man, this story will offer encouragement:

•

Carol Rosen

From Frogs to the Prince

I had to write to you because I've had more than my share of jerks. How many? There were Stan and Mike, who both left me for other women. And there was Steve, my first love, who promised to marry me when he got out of the service. Then he walked away because he wasn't ready. His rejection made me feel deeply depressed, and even suicidal.

I took a long break from men after Steve, but then I made the mistake of getting involved with Phil. He didn't like to kiss me and said he couldn't enjoy making love to me until I lost weight. He finally left. I was just a little too chunky for his taste.

Pretty sad list, isn't it? I thought I was doomed, that I'd never meet Mr. Right.

Then I met Don and fell for him like a ton of bricks. I was scared to death that history would repeat itself. But guess what? He fell for me, too. We married four happy years ago and are still going strong.

Now, as I write this, I can hardly remember all those bad years. At times, I felt there was no reason to go on living. I have one message for women who are with jerks: Leave him before he dumps you. It's not worth it.

•

Maybe He's Just a Jerk

I am not necessarily in favor of taking revenge on men who have hurt you, but I have to admit I felt a small twinge of satisfaction when I heard from women who had turned the tables on their creeps. Tracy wrote to tell me about a man whose track record in affairs with women was a mile long:

> Nick cheated on me whenever he got the chance, and I kept forgiving him. It felt like he had me under a spell; I couldn't stand to be without him. I finally managed to break away, after I discovered he was sleeping with one of my friends. I realized how dangerous it was for me to be in love with this horrible man.
>
> Three weeks after I broke up with him for good, I ran into Nick at a neighborhood tavern. He was drinking heavily and trying to pick up a girl at the bar. I ignored him and sat at a table with friends. I had a lot of fun that night. Finally, it was time to leave. Nick was still at the bar, cozily sitting with his arm around the woman. His next victim! As I passed him, I said to Nick in my sweetest voice, "Be sure to tell her about your herpes!"
>
> Okay, I realize it was a low blow, since Nick didn't have herpes, but you should have seen the look on that woman's face! All is fair in

•

to me that by the time they paid the weekly day-care fee, they had practically no money left. Again, you may be able to get assistance or join a program that has a sliding-scale fee structure. Check with the child-care referral service in your area. Or, if you know women in similar circumstances, you can start a child-care co-op of your own. I've heard from women who have done this.

Once you decide to get a divorce, the first step is to find a lawyer who will help you and your children receive a fair settlement. If you can't afford a lawyer, call the local office of the American Bar Association. It will refer you to a Legal Aid office in your area.

Psychologically, if you are feeling overwhelmed, anxious and depressed, don't be afraid to seek professional help. Many women think they have to bear all their burdens alone. This isn't true. If you can't afford professional help, or your insurance policy doesn't cover it, check with your local social-services agency to see what kind of help is available for little or no cost. You can supplement one-on-one therapy by joining one of the many free or low-cost self-help programs currently available.

The point is: You have options. No woman needs to tolerate abuse of any kind—whether it's physical or emotional. No woman needs to accept endless criticism or cruel barbs. No woman has to be a prisoner to a man who treats her like dirt. As a friend told me

•

when she left her abusive boyfriend, "Hey, women are people, too!" For her, it was a great revelation. It is my dream that the time will come when women will no longer waste their time on dead-end relationships that bring them nothing but misery. We have better things to do with our lives.

•

Where to Find Help

*T*he following national hotlines will advise you about support groups or aid that is available to you locally. They cover a wide range of services and are staffed with competent professionals and caring volunteers whose job it is to help people. I've included hotlines that cater to a number of different issues. While they may not seem directly relevant to relationships, it is often the case that secondary problems can be the partial source of your troubles. Please don't hesitate to call!

•

Appendix A

Battered Women's Hotline
National Coalition Against Domestic Violence
800-333-SAFE

National AIDS Information Center
800-342-2437

National Council on Compulsive Gambling
800-522-4700

National Runaway Switchboard
800-621-4000

National Youth Crisis Hotline
800-448-4663

Parents Anonymous
800-421-0353

Runaway Hotline
(United States, except Texas)
800-231-6946
Texas: 800-392-3352

Self-Help Clearinghouse
800-367-6274

**Sexually Transmitted Diseases (STD)
National Hotline**
800-227-8922

•

Appendix A

Suicide Hotline
800-367-6274

The following groups might also offer you guidance and support. Many of them are based on the successful Twelve-Step approach used by Alcoholics Anonymous.

Adult Children of Alcoholics
P.O. Box 3216
2522 W. Sepulveda Blvd., Suite 200
Torrance, CA 90505
213-534-1815

Adult Children of Alcoholics is a Twelve-Step group for people whose parents were (are) alcoholics or who come from other dysfunctional family situations—drug abusers, incest survivors, etc.

Al-Anon
P.O. Box 862
Midtown Station
New York, NY 10018-0862
212-302-7240

Al-Anon helps spouses, relatives, friends or significant others of alcoholics. It is an international organization with approximately thirty thousand groups.

•

215

Appendix A

Alateen
P.O. Box 862
Midtown Station
New York, NY 10018-0862
212-302-7240

This is an Al-Anon group for teenagers whose parent(s) are alcoholics or substance abusers.

Alcoholics Anonymous
P.O. Box 454
Grand Central Station
New York, NY 10017
212-686-1100

AA is available in most communities as a recovery program for alcoholics who have a desire to stop drinking.

Anxiety Disorder Association of America
600 Executive Blvd., Suite 200
Rockville, MD 20852-3801
301-231-9350

This organization addresses the needs of persons who suffer from anxiety disorders such as a high generalized level of anxiety, panic attacks and phobias.

•

Appendix A

Association for Children for Enforcement of Support (ACES)
723 Phillips Avenue
Toledo, OH 43612
800-537-7072

This organization provides free information on how to get child support. It provides general and specific information related to your case. Best of all, its services are free.

Co-Anon
P.O. Box 64742-66
Los Angeles, CA 90064
213-859-2206

Co-Anon is a Twelve-Step group for spouses, friends or significant others of cocaine abusers.

Cocaine Anonymous
World Service Office
3740 Overland Avenue, Suite G
Los Angeles, CA 90032
213-559-5833
800-347-8998

Cocaine Anonymous is a Twelve-Step group that offers hope and recovery to cocaine users who wish to stop.

•

Appendix A

Co-Dependents Anonymous (CoDa)
P.O. Box 33577
Phoenix, AZ 85067-3577
602-277-7991

CoDa is a Twelve-Step group that helps men and women maintain functional relationships. It is helpful for those who exert most of their energy trying to "fix" others' or their relationships at the expense of their own needs.

Codependents of Sex Addicts (CoSa)
P.O. Box 14537
Minneapolis, MN 55414
612-537-6904

CoSa is a recovery program for people who are married to or who "enable" sex addicts. Both men and women may attend meetings, although some meetings are gender-separated. The anonymity of members is carefully protected.

Emotions Anonymous (EA)
P.O. Box 4245
St. Paul, MN 55104
612-647-9712

EA helps people recover from a variety of emotional disorders, including anger, grief, guilt, depression, anxiety and phobias.

•

Appendix A

Families Anonymous (FA)
P.O. Box 528
Van Nuys, CA 91408
818-989-7841

FA is organized to address severe family crises, usually involving substance abuse. It is especially useful for addressing substance abuse and eating disorders in children and teenagers.

Gam-Anon
P.O. Box 157
Whitestone, NY 11357
718-352-1671

Gam-Anon offers hope and recovery to the families of compulsive gamblers.

Gamblers Anonymous
P.O. Box 17173
Los Angeles, CA 90017
213-386-8789

This organization is designed to help people overcome a debilitating addiction to gambling.

Hazelden Foundation
P.O. Box 176
Pleasant Valley Road
Center City, MN 55012
800-328-9000

•

This organization provides pamphlets, books and other materials for the recognition, prevention, understanding of and recovery from chemical dependency in adherence to the Alcoholics Anonymous Twelve-Step philosophy.

Incest Survivors Anonymous (ISA)
P.O. Box 5613
Long Beach, CA 90805-0613
310-428-5599

ISA addresses the impact of childhood sexual abuse and enables those who have suffered it to become survivors in adulthood.

Nar-Anon
P.O. Box 2562
Palos Verdes, CA 90274
213-547-5800

Nar-Anon is a Twelve-Step support group, similar to Al-Anon but specifically for those dealing with narcotic addiction in a family member, friend or loved one.

Narcotics Anonymous
P.O. Box 9999
Van Nuys, CA 91409
818-780-3951

•

Appendix A

Narcotics Anonymous is a Twelve-Step program that offers hope and recovery to addicts who wish to stop using drugs.

National Coalition Against Domestic Violence
1500 Massachusetts Ave. N.W., Suite 15
Washington, DC 20005
800-333-SAFE

This organization provides a hotline that refers women to local shelters and places where they can get counseling if they are the victims of domestic violence. It also provides literature by mail.

National Coalition Against Sexual Assault
P.O. Box 7156
Austin, TX 78712
512-472-8858

Call this organization for referrals to rape crisis centers in your area. Rape crisis centers will counsel victims of both recent rapes and those that occurred in the past. They also help people deal with "date rape" and rape that happens within marriage.

O-Anon
P.O. Box 4350
San Pedro, CA 90731
(no phone number)

•

O-Anon is a Twelve-Step group for the family and friends of compulsive overeaters. It helps people understand all aspects of the disease, including obesity, anorexia and bulimia.

Overeaters Anonymous
P.O. Box 92870
Los Angeles, CA 90009
213-542-8363

OA is a Twelve-Step group that offers help and recovery to persons who are addicted to food and/ or are having problems with obesity, binge eating, anorexia, bulimia and other eating disorders.

Parents Anonymous
22330 Hawthorne
Torrance, CA 90505
(no phone number)

Parents Anonymous offers counseling and support for families in which one or both parents are physically and/or sexually abusive toward their children.

Parents United
Daughters United
Sons United
P.O. Box 952
San Jose, CA 95108
408-453-7616

•

Appendix A

Parents United is a support group for couples in which one partner has sexually abused a child.

Daughters United and Sons United are support groups for the male and female victims of incest.

S-Anon
P.O. Box 5117
Sherman Oaks, CA 91413
818-990-6901

This is a support group for the family and friends of sex addicts.

Sex Addicts Anonymous
P.O. Box 3038
Minneapolis, MN 95403
612-339-0217

SAA is a Twelve-Step program that offers hope and recovery for persons who suffer from the disease of sexual addiction.

Sexaholics Anonymous
P.O. Box 300
Simi Valley, CA 93062
805-581-3343

•

Appendix A

Sexaholics Anonymous also offers support for people who are suffering from sex addictions.

Survivors of Incest Anonymous (SIA)
P.O. Box 21817
Baltimore, MD 21222-6817
301-282-3400

SIA is for persons over the age of eighteen who were sexually abused as children.

Smokers Anonymous
2118 Greenwich St.
San Francisco, CA 94123

This is a support and referral program for people who have decided to kick their smoking habit.

Stepfamily Association of America
28 Allegheny Ave., Suite 1307
Baltimore, MD 21204
301-823-7570

This organization provides information on local chapters and issues a newsletter for step-families.

If none of these organizations addresses your problem, you can write to the following organization for further information:

•

Appendix A

Alliance of Information and Referral Services
1100 W. 42nd St., Suite 310
Indianapolis, IN 46208
(no phone number)

I would also love to hear from you if you have a story to share or comments about the book. You can write to me at:

JERK
P.O. Box 277
Calumet City, IL 60409

.

Appendix B

·

Reading List

The following books can be helpful as you work toward making your life jerk free.

Beattie, Melody. *Codependent No More*. Center City, MN: The Hazelden Foundation, 1987.
    This book is fantastic for people (especially women) who are so busy taking care of everyone else that they never have time for their own needs. Although many people believe the term "codependent" applies only to the spouse or loved one of a substance abuser, it can be broadly applied

·

to anyone who is so obsessed with controlling another person's behavior that they ignore their own needs.

Berliner-Statman, Jan. *The Battered Woman's Survival Guide*. Dallas, TX: Taylor Publishing Co., 1990.
This is a wonderful new resource for battered women and their families and friends. It explains the cycle of violence and includes an excellent checklist that will help you spot (and avoid) a Batterer. The author also explains how "learned helplessness" keeps women locked in hellish relationships. There is a directory of referrals.

Black, Claudia. *It Will Never Happen to Me*. Denver, CO: M.A.C., 1982.
This is a very good book for adult children of alcoholics and other kinds of dysfunctional families. It also addresses circumstances faced by spouses and children of current substance abusers.

Bolles, Richard. *What Color Is Your Parachute?—A Practical Manual for Job-Hunters and Career Changers*. Berkeley, CA: Ten Speed Press, 1982.
This book has been the job-hunter's bible for many years. If you've never worked outside the home, it will help you discover your special talents and abilities. It includes many creative job-hunting techniques as well.

Burns, Dr. David. *Feeling Good*. New York: William Morrow, Inc., 1980.
Although this book was written for people who suffer

•

from depression, it may be useful if you're with a jerk. It contains very good exercises that will help you view the world and your life in a more positive light. The author includes excellent practical advice on how to raise your self-esteem.

Drews, Toby Rice. *Getting Them Sober: Volumes One and Two*. Los Angeles: Bridge Pub., 1980.

If you are living with an alcoholic or drug abuser, think of these two books as survival manuals. The author gives practical advice on such subjects as "No More Taking the Blame for His Drinking" and "No More Lying to His Boss."

Engel, Beverly, MFCC. *The Emotionally Abused Woman— Overcoming Destructive Patterns and Reclaiming Yourself*. Los Angeles: Lowell Hse, RGA Publishing Group, 1990.

This is an excellent book if you are with a Critic. It explains how to tell if you're being abused, the types of emotional abusers and how "unfinished business" from your youth may be affecting you today.

Forward, Dr. Susan, with Craig Buck. *Toxic Parents— Overcoming Their Hurtful Legacy and Reclaiming Your Life*. New York: Bantam Books, 1989.

This is a great book for anyone who comes from a dysfunctional family. The authors describe how your parents may have hurt you, physically or emotionally, as a child, and how those experiences affect you today.

•

Forward, Dr. Susan, and Joan Torres. *Men Who Hate Women and the Women Who Love Them—When Loving Hurts and You Don't Know Why.* New York: Bantam, 1986.

This book is a great resource for women with jerks— especially the Critic. You'll learn why women stay with them, how they "hook" you and how they take control. The authors also examine patterns of destructive relationships and provide exercises to help you build your self-esteem.

Geringer-Wotitz, Janet, Ed.D. *Adult Children of Alcoholics.* Deerfield Beach, FL: Health Communications, Inc., 1983.

This book is considered a classic in its field. It explains the patterns children of alcoholics learn in order to survive in troubled family environments, and how these patterns affect you in adulthood. It also gives a strong sense of hope for change and happiness.

Halpern, Howard M., Ph.D. *How to Break Your Addiction to a Person.* New York: Bantam, 1983.

This book is helpful to you whether or not you're in an "addictive" relationship. What's an addictive relationship? One that isn't good for you but that you can't stand to break off. The author describes the factors that keep you a "prisoner of love," and, most important, how to leave a bad relationship and keep your sanity.

Kuriansky, Judy. *How to Love a Nice Guy.* New York: Doubleday, 1990.

This is a very readable guide to the dynamics that keep

•

you attracted to jerks. Especially powerful are the sections "Recognize Your Personal Power," "Wake Up to Emotional Traps," and "Recognize Family Dramas and Scripts—How to Stop Reenacting the Ones That Don't Work."

Maltz, Dr. Maxwell. *Pyscho-Cybernetics.* New York: Pocket Books, 1960.

This old favorite has been in print for more than thirty years, but its advice is still fresh and useful. While it doesn't deal specifically with personal relationships, I've included it because I found it helpful in my own self-improvement and positive-thinking efforts. This is one of the best books I've read on how your mind works, how to build a better self-image and how to realize your fullest potential.

NiCarthy, Ginny. *Getting Free: A Handbook for Women in Abusive Relationships.* Seattle: Seal Press, 1982.

This is an excellent resource for battered women that gives compassionate and practical advice on how to start a new and safe life. It has been highly recommended by the Illinois Coalition Against Domestic Violence.

———. *The Ones Who Get Away—Women Who Left Abusive Partners.* Seattle: Seal Press, 1987.

If you have been or are now in an abusive relationship of any kind, this book will be a true inspiration. It includes numerous case studies from women of every age, race, religion and socioeconomic group that tell how they freed themselves of abusive partners and are leading happy, safe lives today.

•

Norwood, Robin. *Women Who Love Too Much: When You Keep Wishing and Hoping He'll Change.* Los Angeles: J. P. Tarcher, 1985.

Whether you've had one or a series of bad relationships, the author suggests you may have a "relationship addiction"—comparable to alcohol addiction. This is a helpful, inspiring and moving book, filled with women's stories and good advice. Once you read it, I guarantee you'll understand better why you get involved with jerks.

Russianoff, Dr. Penelope. *Why Do I Think I'm Nothing Without a Man?* New York: Bantam, 1985.

This book shows that you can have a great life without a man. The author explores the reasons so many of us think we are worthless without a man in our lives, and how our society reinforces this notion. She gives good advice about how to lead a fulfilling life by forming a network of male and female friends, pursuing your career and taking care of your own needs. By doing this, you can become happily and healthily single, and you'll be more open to pursuing a good relationship, if one presents itself.

Schaef, Anne Wilson. *Co-Dependence: Mistreated, Misunderstood.* San Francisco: Harper & Row, 1986.

This is one of the pioneering books in the field of co-dependency. The author shows how you can be addicted to a relationship, how widespread such addictions are and how society condones the addiction. She tells how both men and women can fall into the codependency trap.

•

Shiromoto, Frank N., and Edgar F. Soren. *Drugs and Drinks—Painful Questions: How Substance Abusers and Their Loved Ones Ask for Help.* Monterey, CA: Choices Press, 1988.

This is an excellent small book that covers substance abuse and its effect on spouses and children. It is written in an easy-to-read question-and-answer format, with quizzes to help you determine if you or your spouse are drug or alcohol dependent.

Turner, Tina, with Kurt Loder. *I, Tina.* New York: Avon, 1987.

Here is an entertaining and deeply inspirational book about the popular singer's long years with an abusive spouse. Turner describes how her husband, Ike, abused her physically and emotionally for years and how she finally escaped. For those of you who think your circumstances are special, this is a real eye-opener. Abuse can happen to anybody!

Walker, Dr. Lenore. *The Battered Woman.* New York: Harper & Row, 1977.

This book offers a vivid description of the horrors that occur in a battering relationship. The author describes how the abuse cycle works and how a battered woman compensates. Best of all, she gives advice for getting free.

•

Index

AA (Alcoholics Anonymous), 186
   Con Man and, 54
abortion, 123, 126
Addict, 29–30, 175–190
   children of, 179–180, 183–
      184, 187–189, 194
   codependency (enabling) and,
      178–179, 186, 187
   denial in, 177
   difficulties in identification of,
      177–178
   exposing of, 189–190
   habit hidden by, 178
   multiple addictions of, 185

reasons for involvement with,
   184
sex and, 185–186
and societal attitudes toward
   substance use, 177–
   178
support system of, 178
affairs:
   with married men, *see* Mar-
      ried Seducer
   see also infidelity
aid, hotlines for finding, 213–
   224
Al-Anon, 188

•

Index

alcohol abuse, 201
  by Batterer, 158, 160
  excuses for, 88, 158, 178
  see also Addict
Alcoholics Anonymous (AA), 186
  Con Man and, 54
aloneness, fear of, 21, 196–197
Alternatives to Domestic Aggression, 199
American Bar Association, 210
apologies:
  of Batterer, 155, 160
  of Critic, 49
  of Sleazy Lover, 84
artists, 63
Associated Press, 16

baby-sitting cooperatives, 34
"bait and switch" technique, 198–200
battered women, 175, 192
  shelters for, 158, 170, 171, 173
  signs of abuse of, 159
  statistics on, 152–153, 171
Batterer, 28–29, 151–173
  disbelief of outsiders and, 153, 166–170
  familiar course of behavior in, 156
  legal action against, 167–171
  nice-guy pose as trap of, 153, 199
  reasons women stay with, 172–173
  social prominence and, 166–167
  typical cycle of, 154–156
  warning signs of, 156–158
belittling, 42–43
blaming and fault-finding:
  by Batterer, 28–29, 171–172

  by mother-in-law, 176
  of oneself, for bad relationship, 15, 17, 22, 32
  of oneself, for parents' abuse, 194–195
  see also Critic
books, self-help, 15, 16, 112
  reading list of, 227–233
bullying, 32, 44–47, 48, 152
Bundy, Ted, 154

call girls, 73–74
cancer, 48, 78–79
Catholic Social Services, 199
charm:
  of Batterer, 153, 154
  of Con Man, 25, 51, 53, 67
  of Critic, 45
Charming Scoundrel, 26–27, 97–112
  attachment to past in, 105–107
  excuses made by, 99, 111, 112
  marriage promise as ploy of, 109–110
  pursuit followed by uninterest from, 102–104
  relationship terminated by, 104–105
  walking away from, 111–112
  wedding date postponed by, 107–109
cheapskates, 62
cheating, *see* infidelity
child care, 208, 209–210
children:
  abuse of, 169, 195, 209
  of addicts, 179–180, 183–184, 187–189, 194
  effects of divorce on, 80
  financial assistance and, 209
  self-blame in, 194–195

•

•

Index

•

•